THREE PLAYS

CHRISTOPHER FRY

THREE PLAYS:

The Firstborn
Thor, with Angels
A Sleep of Prisoners

A Galaxy Book

NEW YORK
OXFORD UNIVERSITY PRESS
1965

CONTENTS

FOREWORD

THE three plays brought together in this volume, and *The Boy with a Cart*, which is not included here, fall easily into the category Religious, as distinct from the comedies, which more than once have been called Pagan. But if any are religious they are all religious, and if any are pagan they are all pagan. They reflect the world I know, as far as my understanding has taken me.

The real difference is that the comedies were written to be played in a theatre; the others either in, or not far away from, a church. Even *The Firstborn* was begun as a play to be performed outside Tewkesbury Abbey. It may be possible to notice how it changes its pace, and becomes more enclosed, at the point when this project was abandoned.

Thor, with Angels was written for the Chapter House of Canterbury Cathedral. This meant performance on an open stage, and partly accounts for Merlin's long speech on p. 145. In the theatre this speech brings the action of the play to a standstill. It marks a passage of time; and in the Chapter House there was no curtain to divide one scene from another. The speech, therefore, takes the place of interval music and it carries us across from the morning to the evening.

It serves, also, two or three other purposes. It gives Hoel a dream while he lies sleeping on the stage; and it presents a theme, which isn't only part of the content of *Thor*, but of the comedies as well; the theme of the evolutionary adventure which man is engaged on. Life—mineral, vegetable, animal—is one, and, in a sense, our ultimate goal was contained in the rock. The word had been sent out; the exploration initiated.

We seem to pursue this secret mission inevitably, though it is not apparent to our minds, and seems to bear some comparison with the pursuit of the shape of the butterfly by the caterpillar, and (in the human being) with the pursuit of form by the musician or the poet. There is, I think, in the artist a sense of something being there before the work is begun—something, I mean, different from the 'idea'—which is not capable of being stated, and may only partially be achieved.

It is in this context that I find the human being particularly interesting, though it would take more ability than mine to express it clearly. In the comedies, I know, the characters have some difficulty in making themselves heard above the chorus of mineral, vegetable, and animal. Fish swim through the walls, as they did through the reflection of Mendip's castle. Nevertheless it is a view of man which I believe to be true, and worth trying to get down on paper, even if the likeness fails. It concerns every aspect of our lives, material, moral, spiritual; and good and evil become literally life and death, what continues the progression, or what halts it; growth or ossification.

Merlin is so devoted to his unity with all created things that he can hardly distinguish, he says, 'the storm-swollen river from the tear-swollen eyes, Or the bare cracked earth from the burnt-out face, Or the forest soughing from the sighing heart'. And, in full knowledge of what he is doing, he prefers to remain at that stage, while Cymen is forced on to more fearful steps in the progression. Jennet, in *The Lady's Not For Burning*, takes Merlin's sense of unity with all created things, and converts it into choice:

> What is deep, as love is deep, I'll have
> Deeply. What is good, as love is good,
> I'll have well. Then if time and space
> Have any purpose, I shall belong to it.

But if I go on underlining these points I shall make the plays sound like philosophical propositions, which they are not; and there would be no need to say a word in explanation if we weren't so ready to reduce ourselves to psychological automata, rather than to

[viii]

know ourselves as movement on the road of increasing consciousness. This is what Peter Able, in *A Sleep of Prisoners*, is saying when he prays:

> Deal me high, deal me low.
> Make my deeds
> My nameless needs.
> I know I do not know.

And it is one of the reasons why something of our nature expresses itself in verse, obedient to form. The conflict in dramatic verse is the tussle between this obedience and the anarchy of common speech, which exist together like necessity and free-will.

17 *March* 1960

THE FIRSTBORN

A Play in Three Acts

First published by the Cambridge University Press 1946,
reissued by the Oxford University Press 1949,
Second edition February 1952, Third edition 1958

To

MY MOTHER
and
MY BROTHER

FOREWORD

THIS play—begun as long ago as 1938, though not finished until 1945 after four years when circumstance made me neglect it—has a title which at first may seem to quarrel with most of the action, since the chief protagonist is Moses. But I hope, after a little acquaintance, the figure of life which Rameses presents will be seen to take a central place from his first entrance to the end. The character of Moses is a movement towards maturity, towards a balancing of life within the mystery, where the conflicts and dilemmas are the trembling of the balance. In the last scene he suffers a momentary spiritual death ('I followed a light into a blindness') at the moment when the firstborn's physical death creates the Hebrews' freedom; and his resurrection from that, to become the great leader, though only hinted at as the curtain falls, carries with it something of the life of Rameses.

> Death was their question to us, and our lives
> Become their understanding or perplexity.
> And by living to answer them, we also answer
> Our own impermanence.

Rameses lives a boyhood almost identical with Moses' own; he and the Hebrew Shendi between them draw the frontiers of combat altogether differently from the lines laid down by accepted human action. Rameses is the innocence, humanity, vigour, and worth which stand on the enemy side, not altering the justice or necessity of Moses' cause, but linking the ways of men and the ways of God with a deep and urgent question-mark.

I made certain alterations and cuts immediately after the Edinburgh Festival production in 1948; and for this edition I have revised those alterations, refashioned the last scene, and cut further. This is

[5]

a welcome opportunity to say how much I was helped, in the play's early stages, by the encouragement of Gerard Hopkins and the late Charles Williams; and by Frank Kendon, of the Cambridge University Press, whose belief in it, in 1946, first saw it into print.

C. F.

28 *December* 1951

NOTE TO THE THIRD EDITION

This edition of *The Firstborn* incorporates alterations which made for the New York production (April 1958) which, later in the same year, visited Tel Aviv on the occasion of the tenth anniversary of the founding of the State of Israel.

A play can be a fairly fluid affair, taking new turns in the hands of different actors. In making the present version I was much helped by the imaginative penetration of Anthony Quayle who both played the part of Moses and directed the production.

C. F.

June 1958

THE FIRSTBORN

Gateway Theatre, Edinburgh, 6 September 1948

Anath Bithiah	ATHENE SEYLER
Teusret	DEIRDRE DOONE
Seti the Second	ROBERT SPEAIGHT
Rameses	PAUL HANSARD
Moses	IVAN BRANDT
Aaron	ROBERT SANSOM
Miriam	HENZIE RAEBURN
Shendi	ROBERT RIETTY

Directed by E. Martin Browne

Winter Garden Theatre, London, 29 January 1952

Anath Bithiah	BARBARA EVEREST
Teusret	RUTH TROUNCER
Seti the Second	MARK DIGNAM
Rameses	TONY BRITTON
Moses	ALEC CLUNES
Aaron	CYRIL LUCKHAM
Miriam	DOROTHY REYNOLDS
Shendi	ROBERT RIETTY

Directed by John Fernald

Coronet Theatre, New York, 30 April 1958

Anath Bithiah	KATHARINE CORNELL
Teusret	KATHLEEN WIDDOES
Seti the Second	TORIN THATCHER
Rameses	ROBERT DRIVAS
Moses	ANTHONY QUAYLE
Aaron	MICHAEL STRONG
Miriam	MILDRED NATWICK
Shendi	MICHAEL WAGER

Directed by Anthony Quayle

[7]

CHARACTERS
IN THE ORDER OF THEIR APPEARANCE

ANATH BITHIAH, *Pharaoh's sister*

TEUSRET, *Pharaoh's daughter*

SETI THE SECOND, *the Pharaoh*

RAMESES, *his son*

MOSES

AARON, *his brother*

MIRIAM, *his sister*

SHENDI, *Miriam's son*

Two overseers, a Minister (KEF)

A guard and a servant

The action of the play takes place in the summer of 1200 B.C., alternating between Pharaoh's palace and Miriam's tent

[8]

ACT ONE

SCENE ONE

The terrace of the palace of Seti the Second, at Tanis. A morning in the summer of 1200 B.C. A flight of steps (unseen) leads down through a gate to open ground. The terrace looks out upon an incompleted pyramid.

A scream.

Enter from the palace ANATH BITHIAH, *a woman of fifty, sister to the Pharaoh, and* TEUSRET, *a girl of fifteen, the Pharaoh's daughter*

ANATH. What was it, Teusret?

TEUSRET. Did you hear it too?

ANATH. Some man is dead. That scream was password to a grave.
Look there: up go the birds!

TEUSRET. The heat on this terrace!
You could bake on these stones, Aunt Anath.

ANATH. Ask who it was.

TEUSRET. They're working steadily at father's tomb.
There's no sign of trouble.

ANATH. We're too far off to see.
We should know more if we could see their faces.

TEUSRET [*calling down the steps*]. Guard! Come up here.

ANATH. I should like to be certain.
Oh, that pyramid! Everyday, watching it build,
Will make an old woman of me early.
It will cast a pretty shadow when it's done.
Two hundred more men were taken on today,
Did you know that, Teusret? Your father's in a hurry.

[9]

Their sweat would be invaluable to the farmers in this drought.
What pains they take to house a family of dust.

TEUSRET. It's a lovely tomb.

ANATH.   Yes, so it may be.
But what shall we do with all that air to breathe
And no more breath? I could as happily lie
And wait for eternal life in something smaller

Enter A GUARD

TEUSRET. What was that scream we heard?

GUARD.   It's nothing, madam.

ANATH. You are right. Nothing. It was something once
But now it is only a scare of birds in the air
And a pair of women with their nerves uncovered;
Nothing.

TEUSRET. Who was it screamed?

GUARD.   One of the builders
Missed his footing, madam; merely an Israelite.
They're digging him into the sand. No, over to the left.

TEUSRET. Oh yes, I see them now.—That was all I wanted.

[*Exit* THE GUARD
So that 's all right.

ANATH.   Can you remember your cousin?

TEUSRET. Why, which cousin?

ANATH.   My foster son. You knew him
When you were little. He lived with us in the palace.

TEUSRET. The birds are back on the roof now.

ANATH.   Moses, Teusret.

TEUSRET. What, Aunt? Yes, I think I remember. I remember
 A tall uncle. Was he only a cousin?
 He used to drum his helmet with a dagger
 While he sang us regimental marches to get us to sleep.
 It never did. Why?

ANATH.　　　　　　　　No reason. I thought of him.
 Well, they've buried the man in the sand. We'd better
 Find our morning again and use what's left.

TEUSRET. Why did you think of him? Why *then* particularly?

ANATH. Why not then? Sometimes he blows about my brain
 Like litter at the end of a public holiday.
 I have obstinate affections. Ask your father.
 He would tell you, if it wasn't impolitic
 To mention Moses, what a girl of fire
 I was, before I made these embers.
 He could tell you how I crossed your grandfather,
 And your grandfather was a dynasty in himself.
 Oh Teusret, what a day of legend that was!
 I held forbidden Israel in my arms
 And growled on my stubborn doorstep, till I had my way.

TEUSRET. What do you mean?

ANATH.　　　　　　　　Well, never mind.

TEUSRET.　　　　　　　　　　　　　　I do.
 You've told me so far.

ANATH.　　　　　　　Keep it to yourself then.
 The summer of '24 had brilliant days
 And unprecedented storms. The striped linen
 You once cut up for a doll's dress was the dress
 Made for me that summer. It was the summer
 When my father, your grandfather, published the pronounce-
　　ment.

[11]

TEUSRET. What pronouncement?

ANATH.   That all the boys of Jewdom
Should be killed. Not out of spite, Teusret; necessity.
Your grandfather ordered that Defence of the Realm be painted
At the head of the document, in azure and silver.
It made it easier for him.

TEUSRET.   Were they killed?

ANATH. Yes, they all died of a signature. Or we thought so,
Until the thirtieth of August. I went bathing on that day.
I was a girl then, Teusret, and played with the Nile
As though with a sister. And afterwards as I waded
To land again, pushing the river with my knees,
The wash rocked a little ark out
Into the daylight: and in the ark I found
A tiny weeping Israel who had failed
To be exterminated. When I stooped
With my hair dripping on to his face
He stopped in a screwed-up wail and looked.
And when I found my hands and crowded him
Into my breast, he buried like a burr.
And when I spoke I laughed, and when I laughed
I cried, he was so enchanting. I was ready
To raise a hornet's nest to keep him; in fact
I raised one. All the court flew up and buzzed.
But what could they do? Not even my Pharaoh-father
Could sting him out of my arms. So he grew up
Into your tall cousin, Egyptian
From beard to boots and, what was almost better,
A soldier of genius. You don't remember
How I held you on this terrace, to see him come home from war?
It was ten years ago. Do you remember

[12]

The shrieking music, and half Egypt shouting
Conqueror! Peacemaker!

TEUSRET.   No.

ANATH.   They have all tried to forget.
They have blotted him out of the records, but not out
Of my memory.

TEUSRET.   Why did they blot him out?

ANATH. I might have known that I should say too much.

TEUSRET. Aunt, you must tell me.

ANATH.   Well, no doubt I meant to.
The day I held you here, he came as the conqueror
Of Abyssinia. In all the windows and doors
Women elbowed and cracked their voices; and men
Hung on the gates and the trees; and children sang
The usual songs, conducted by their teachers.

TEUSRET. Yes, but what happened to make him——

ANATH. All right, I'm coming to it, Teusret. The day after,
For the country-side also to be able to see the hero,
He went to inspect the city being built at Pithom.—
My book was closed from that day forward.
He went round with an officer who unfortunately
Was zealous but unintelligent. Silly man:
Silly, silly man. He found a labourer
Idling or resting, and he thought, I suppose,
'I'll show this prince that I'm worth my position'
And beat the workman. A Jewish bricklayer.
He beat him senseless.

TEUSRET.   And then?

ANATH. Moses turned—turned to what was going on—
Turned himself and his world turtle. It was
As though an inward knife scraped his eyes clean.

[13]

The General of Egypt, the Lion and the Prince
Recognized his mother's face in the battered body
Of a bricklayer; saw it was not the face above
His nursery, not my face after all.
He knew his seed. And where my voice had hung till then
Now voices descending from ancestral Abraham
Congregated on him. And he killed
His Egyptian self in the self of that Egyptian
And buried that self in the sand.

TEUSRET.   Aunt—

Enter A GUARD

GUARD.   The Pharaoh.
Madam, the Pharaoh is here.

ANATH.   Can we look innocent?

Enter SETI. *Exit* THE GUARD

TEUSRET. Good morning, father.

SETI.   Go indoors, my Teusret.

                                    [*Exit* TEUSRET

Where is Moses?

ANATH. Seti!

SETI.   Where is Moses? You will know.
In what country? Doing what?

ANATH.   Why Moses?

SETI. I need him.

ANATH.   I've no reason to remember.
I'm without him.

SETI.   But you know.

[14]

ANATH.   Why should I know?
   Why should I? When the sun goes down do I have to know
   Where and how it grovels under the world?
   I thought he was a dust-storm we had shut outside.
   Even now I sometimes bite on the grit.

SETI. I have found him necessary.
   Libya is armed along the length of her frontier,
   And the South's like sand, shifting and uncertain.
   I need Moses.—We have discarded in him
   A general of excellent perception.

ANATH. He's discarded, rightly or wrongly. We've let him go.

SETI. Deeds lie down at last, and so did his.
   Out in the wilderness, after two days' flight,
   His deed lay down, knowing what it had lost him.
   Under the boredom of thorn-trees he cried out
   For Egypt and his deed died. Ten years long
   He has lugged this dead thing after him.
   His loyalty needn't be questioned.

ANATH. We're coming to something strange when a normal day
   Opens and lets in the past. He may remember
   Egypt. He's in Midian.

SETI.   In what part of Midian?

ANATH. Wherever buckets are fetched up out of wells
   Or in his grave.

SETI.   We'll find him. If we have to comb
   Midian to its shadows we'll find him.

ANATH.   He's better where he is.

SETI. He is essential to my plans.

ANATH. I tell you
He is better where he is. For you or me
He's better where he is.
We have seen different days without him
And I have done my hair a different way.
Leave him alone to bite his lips.

[SETI'S *eye is caught by something below and beyond the terrace*

SETI. What's this,
What is this crowd?

ANATH. It's Rameses! No qualms
For the dynasty, with a son as popular as he is.

SETI. There's half the city round him. Where are his guards?

ANATH. There: a little behind.

SETI. The boy's too careless.
I'm not altogether at rest in the way he's growing,
His good graces for no-matter-whom.
He must learn to let the needs of Egypt rule him.

ANATH. He will learn. He is learning.

SETI. Egypt should pray so.

ANATH. I would hazard a guess that Egypt's women
Have prayed for him often enough. Ra, raising
An eyebrow stiff with the concentration of creation
Probably says: That boy again? We'd better
Make something of him early and have them satisfied.
O, Rameses will be all right.

SETI. I hope,
I hope.

Enter RAMESES, *a boy of eighteen*

RAMESES. Did you see the excitement? I think it's the drought.
Like the air, we're all quivering with heat.

[16]

Do you find that, Aunt? Either you must sleep like the dead
Or something violent must happen.

ANATH.   Look: your father.

RAMESES. I didn't see you, father. I'm sorry, sir.
Did I interrupt state matters?

SETI.   What morning have you had?

RAMESES. Holiday—books rolled up, military exercises
Over, and no social engagements. I've been fowling
Down at the marshes.

ANATH.   Any luck?

RAMESES.   Not much flesh
But a paradise of feathers. I was out before daybreak.

ANATH. It's a good marksman who hunts by batlight.

RAMESES.   But I
Waited for daylight. Until then the marsh was a torpor.
I clucked and clapped as the sun rose
And up shot so much whistle and whirr
I could only hold my spear and laugh.
All the indignant wings of the marshes
Flocking to the banner of Tuesday
To avoid the Prince of Egypt!
Off they flapped into the mist
Looking about for Monday
The day they had lived in peace: and finding nothing
Back they wheeled to Tuesday.
I had recovered myself by then and killed
One that had the breast of a chestnut.
At last he could feel the uninterrupted darkness
Of an addled egg. I watched his nerves flinching
As they felt how dark that darkness was.
I found myself trying to peer into his death.

It seemed a long way down. The morning and it
Were oddly separate,
Though the bird lay in the sun: separate somehow
Even from contemplation.

ANATH.   Excellent spirits
To make a success of a holiday.

RAMESES.   Only for a moment.

SETI. This afternoon I have business for you.   [*He turns to go in*

RAMESES.   Very well.

SETI. Was that thunder?

ANATH.   They're dumping new stone for the
                                                    pyramid.

RAMESES. Two men came through the marshes before I left;
Jews, but not our Jews: or one of them
Was not; he seemed a man of authority
Although some miles of sun and dust were on him.

SETI. Aliens?

RAMESES.   Yes; but one of them I felt
I should have known. How could I?
I passed them again as I came home. They stood
To watch the crowd. I looked across and smiled
But got no smiles from them. And one, the tall one——

ANATH. Very tall?

RAMESES.   Yes, he was tall. It was he
Who is somehow in my memory.

ANATH.   Seti——

SETI.   Well?

ANATH. Is it possible that someone hasn't waited to be recalled?
Is it possible?

[18]

SETI.   It is not possible.

ANATH. Your thoughts are leaning that way too.
Sometimes the unaccountable stalks in.

SETI. Which way were they travelling, Rameses?

RAMESES. This way. If I had only thought of them sooner
We could have seen them go by.—Sir!
They are standing here at the foot of the stairway. How long
Can they have been there? Shall I speak to them?

ANATH. He has stood all day under my brain's stairway.
Seti, who is there? Which foremost, Rameses?
The tall one?

RAMESES.   Yes. Who's in your mind?

ANATH.   The tall one.
The tall one.

                    [RAMESES *goes down the steps*
            So he is back; and small-talk
Has to block a draught up ten years old.

SETI. Why has he come?

ANATH.   You said he longed for Egypt.

SETI. I think so.

ANATH.   But what am I in Egypt?
A dead king's daughter.

            Re-enter RAMESES, *followed by* MOSES *and* AARON

SETI.   What words can I find to fit
So ghostly a homecoming? Understand you are welcome.
Whatever uncertainty you have can go.
We welcome you. Look who is here.

ANATH. He has seen me. We have looked at one another.

SETI. We'll absolve ourselves of the ten years. Who is this?

MOSES. My brother.

SETI.   I had not heard you had a brother.

ANATH. A brother, a sister—and a mother. All the three.

SETI. I told my sister we must have you back.
  And so we must, and so Egypt must; and it seems
  That we have. You are come promptly at the word, Moses.

MOSES. This is not why I came.

SETI.   You would scarcely foresee it.

MOSES. I am not who you think. I am a stranger.

SETI. Not by a vein or a hair. The past is forgotten.
  You are a prince of Egypt.

MOSES.   The prince of Egypt
  Died the day he fled.

SETI.   What do you mean?

MOSES. That prince of Egypt died. I am the Hebrew
  Smitten out of the shadow of that prince,
  Vomited out of his dry lips, the cry
  Whipped off the sanded tongue of that prince of Egypt.

SETI. What has this long discomfort done for you,
  My friend? It has made you bitter.

MOSES. Why was it you decided to ask me to come back?

SETI. Isn't it time we laid the crippling ghost
  That haunts us? You evidently thought so too
  To come so far.

MOSES.   You've a better reason than that.

SETI. Why should you want reasons when you have come
  On your own initiative? Why are you here?
  I am asking you candidly. Why did you come?

MOSES. My blood heard my blood weeping
　　Far off like the swimming of fear under the sea,
　　The sobbing at night below the garden. I heard
　　My blood weeping. It is here it wept and weeps.
　　It was from here I heard coming this drum of despair,
　　Under your shoes, under your smile, and under
　　The foundations of your tomb. From Egypt.

ANATH. What was it, Seti, that lay down and died?

SETI. Why are you here?

MOSES. 　　　　　　　　To be close to this that up to now
　　Has been a pain in the mind, not yet
　　Possessing the mind, but so increasing
　　It has driven me here, to be in myself the pain,
　　To be the pain's own life.

SETI. 　　　　　　　　Still you haven't
　　Answered my question. Come, what do you want?

MOSES. First, that you should know what you are doing.

SETI. Take care, Moses.

ANATH. 　　　　　　And secondly?

MOSES. 　　　　　　　　　　What can I hope
　　From that until he has understood the first?

SETI. What is this mood you have come in which is so ready
　　To abuse a decent welcome? There is something shipwreck
　　About you that will not do for peaceful places.
　　Steady yourself if we're to understand one another.
　　I am the Pharaoh, Moses, not the young uncle
　　Of the Heliopolis classroom, nor your messroom brother.

[21]

MOSES. A man has more to be than a Pharaoh.
He must dare to outgrow the security
Of partial blindness. I'm not speaking now
To your crown; I'm speaking to your merciless mischief.

SETI. You have coarsened during your exile. What you say
Hasn't even the virtue of clarity. If you wish
To consider my offer of reinstatement, go
And consider. I can be patient. Egypt can do
Her work on you like a generous woman, given
Her time.   [*He glances at* ANATH
          Midian will wash off in the Nile.
Go on, go on, I shall not remember this morning.

MOSES. I think you will. My brother has lived these days
In amongst Israel, while I was sleeping.
He knows both the truth and the injury better than I can.
Let him speak what he knows.

AARON. Twelve hundred thousand Israelites are under
Your dominion. Of these two hundred and twenty thousand
Only, are men. The rest are in the proportion
Of four hundred and fifty thousand women
And five hundred and thirty thousand children.

SETI. I have my census-takers.

AARON.   So perhaps
Has Death got his; but I think he has not referred
His undertakings to your dynastic understanding.
Here I have his estimate: between April and July
Six hundred and one deaths suffered in old age
But an old age of forced labour, their backs bent twice,
Under the weight of years and under the mule-whip.
Also thirty-eight deaths of healthy men
Who made some show of reluctance or momentary
Impatience.

[22]

MOSES.   That was a good cure. They are now
  Patient for all eternity.

AARON.   Also the deaths
  Of a hundred pregnant women, forced to dig
  Until they had become their own gravediggers.
  Also the deaths of eighty-four children, twelve
  Unofficial crucifixions . . .

SETI.   This is intolerable
  Singsong! Am I to compose the epitaphs
  For every individual grave of this trying summer?
  I have my figures. I do not need yours.
  I have put men to a purpose who otherwise
  Would have had not the least meaning.

MOSES. Not the least meaning, except the meaning
  Of the breath in your lungs, the mystery of existing
  At all. What have we approached or conceived
  When we have conquered and built a world? Even
  Though civilization became perfect? What then?
  We have only put a crown on the skeleton.
  It is the individual man
  In his individual freedom who can mature
  With his warm spirit the unripe world.
  They are your likeness, these men, even to nightmares.
  I have business with Egypt, one more victory for her,
  A better one than Ethiopia:
  That she should come to see her own shame
  And discover justice for my people.

SETI. You have fermented in your Midian bottle.
  But lately I have learnt an obstinate patience.
  We should have done better to have met
  Out of the sun. We can do better than this
  And so we shall yet, later, at a cooler time.

[23]

Where will you sleep? We will see you have food.
Do you remember, I wonder, the palace nectarine?
I said, where will you lodge?

MOSES.   With my sister, Miriam.

SETI [*to* ANATH]. Do you know where that is?

ANATH.   Perfectly.

SETI [*going in*].   Very well.

ANATH. Now he will not sleep again tonight.

MOSES. I hope that none of us will sleep again
Until we all can sleep.

ANATH.   And so once more
We see each other. You have chosen a fine day.

        [MOSES *waits.* ANATH *says no more. He goes with* AARON

ANATH. I taught him to walk, Rameses. I also taught him
To speak and say his alphabet. I taught you your
Alphabet also; and also Teusret hers.
I have been a really useful woman.

RAMESES.   Where
Does his sister live?

ANATH.   Why do you want to know?

RAMESES. I wondered where it might be.

ANATH.   She has a tent
By the brick-kiln.

RAMESES.   I liked that man.

ANATH. So have others before you. Like him, Rameses,
Forget him, and let us live in peace.

RAMESES. I shall go and find him.

ANATH. Rameses, I ask you to forget him.

[24]

RAMESES. How?

ANATH. What would make it difficult?

RAMESES. Can you forget him?

ANATH. He has gone.

RAMESES. And something of us, I think, went with him.

ANATH. Well, you will let him go. I have asked you.

RAMESES. No.
I love you, you know that. But trust me a little.
I shall be discreet. [*Exit* RAMESES

ANATH. Rameses!—No,
What should I be doing, turning his feet
Towards my fears? [*She goes to the parapet*
Enter TEUSRET

TEUSRET. Aunt Anath, where is Rameses going?
Aunt Anath—

ANATH. Do you remember, Teusret?
A man fell from the pyramid—only this morning.

CURTAIN

SCENE TWO

MIRIAM'S *tent*. MOSES [*in the entrance*]. MIRIAM.

MOSES. Miriam! Miriam!

MIRIAM. Is it my brother? Yes;
You have his immovable look. Aaron told me
To expect you.

MOSES. Can you be Miriam?

[25]

MIRIAM.   A kind
Of residue. Sit down, if you don't mind.
I dislike answering questions. Ask me nothing.
I am very well; I have nothing to offer you
To drink.

MOSES.   I'm glad to be with you after so long.

MIRIAM. You will find it very tiresome after five or six minutes.
I repeat myself unendurably, like the Creation.
Your only hope is to deaden yourself to me
And it.

AARON [*in the entrance*]. Your name runs like fire, like an ostrich!
You didn't wait to hear, but the sergeant at the gate
Was full of it. He said the whole city
Is pulsing with talk and argument about you:
As soon as this; before you've even been seen!

MOSES. And what will this do for us?

AARON.   Surely it suggests
They're taking sides? Down in the square, it seems, a minister's
    wife
Was wearing an M in small lilies; her daughter snatched them off
And threw them among the pigeons. How can Seti
Assure himself what size your faction is?
Egypt loves and hates you inextricably.

MOSES. Egypt is afraid. Love me? No;
They're afraid to be without me.

AARON. That will pass for love.

MOSES. They love me from the bottom of their greed.
Give me the bad news. What men have we lost?

MIRIAM. So you're not only here on a visit to your sister.

AARON. Here is a list. It 's not complete.

MIRIAM.   I've had
  Enough of trouble.

MOSES.   Rahnor, Janeth, Pathrusim—
  Is he lost? Pathrusim? The sand of Egypt
  Is abominably the richer.—Hadoram, Seth,
  Havilah, Dodanim . . .

MIRIAM.   Why do you read
  Dead men's names? There are some of us still breathing.
  Your sister, for example, is still alive,
  Figuratively speaking. I imagined
  You would have plenty to tell me. Have you not?
  Am I always to know nothing of you?

MOSES.   These names are what I am.

MIRIAM. They are yesterday's life. I liked many of them very well;
  But we no longer have anything in common.

AARON. Are we to forget them because we have lost them?

MIRIAM.   To wish
  To be with them comes too easily.

MOSES.   This tent
  Is stifling.

MIRIAM.   I keep it closed. I have no liking
  For what goes on outside.

MOSES.   When do they say
  The mountains last had rain?

MIRIAM.   Nine months ago.

MOSES. It's time for parturition.
  Look: what you shut out is a withering city.
  City of Egypt. This land once I worshipped,
  And now I cannot be sure what I bring against her
  In my heart. This noon, like every other noon,

Still groans with the laborious wheels which drew
The Nile water. There is little difference
Between ourselves and those blindfolded oxen.
We also do the thing we cannot see,
Hearing the creaking pivot and only knowing
That we labour.

MIRIAM.   Why did you bring him? Take yourselves off!
This is my tent, and it's not for restless hands.
He's a dangermaker still.

AARON. What has he said, Miriam?

MIRIAM.   I have a son
And that is all I rest on. There's a man
Who should have been my brother. A king's daughter
Swallowed him and spat out this outlaw. I'll
Not have any more in the family.

AARON.   What should make them?

MIRIAM. You and he. I know. Two years ago
I had it all: the surly men coming in here,
One at a time by signal, hardly nodding
Towards me, covering the table with their knife-cuts
To show how revolution must come, and freedom,
And idiocy; till a beetle striking the lamp
Or the coal settling, would shiver through us all
As though a dagger had sung into the pole.
And Espah and Zoad are dead from it. And you
In a night of loud hyenas went over the border.
Not again. I'll keep my nights of sleep, and I'll keep
My son.

AARON. In this country of murder?

MIRIAM.   I'll keep my son
In whatever country.

MOSES.   Happily?

MIRIAM.   We have
    A way of living. We have the habit. Well?
    It becomes a kind of pleasantness.

MOSES.   You have gone
    With the dead after all, but you pretend not to see them.
    Miriam, we have to speak to them with our lives.
    Death was their question to us, and our lives
    Become their understanding or perplexity.
    And by living to answer them, we also answer
    Our own impermanence. But this rule of Egypt
    Denies us life, Miriam, and gives us nothing
    With which we can outspeak our graves.

MIRIAM.   I am angry;
    The pity is I am angry. I must pretend
    You have said nothing.

AARON.   But do you understand him?
    In fact, do I understand him?

MOSES.   When I was a child,
    Miriam, and you would come to me in the huge
    Nursery of the Pharaohs, we'd go hand
    In hand along your stories, Hebrew stories
    Which like contraband you put quietly in
    To become my nature. Do you remember?

MIRIAM. How she disliked me then! But what a talent
    For condescension she had. I never saw you
    After you were a child except by waiting
    Among the crowd in the streets. There was no need
    To come from Midian to tell me what my life is;
    I have a bowing acquaintance with it. I knew it
    When I hid you to save you from the knives.

[29]

Before I could talk it talked to me
In most difficult words.

MOSES.   What words, Miriam?

MIRIAM. Pogrom, for one. And the curses of Egyptian children
When I ran towards them expecting to play;
The shout of command kicking at the ribs,
All human words torn to a scream.
We have a wildfowl quality of blood,
Moses, temptation for sportsmen.

MOSES.   Go on.

MIRIAM.   With what,
If you please? Do you know the secret which will change
Our spoor? Our grandfather was stoned. I imagine
Creation tried our blood, and brought it in guilty.

MOSES. It was the verdict of Chaos.

MIRIAM.   Let us alone
To serve the sentence. One grows accustomed.
We have to be as we are.

MOSES.   We have
To be Israel; as we are.

MIRIAM. Where do you see Israel now?

MOSES.   Where
Do I see God? Be certain, Israel is.
I am here to be a stone in her sling, out of her gall.

MIRIAM. Israel! Israel's the legend I told you in the nursery.
We've no more spirit to support a God.

MOSES. We have a God who will support the spirit,
And both shall be found. But still I need to know how good
Can be strong enough to break out of the possessing

[30]

Arms of evil. I am there, beyond myself,
If I could reach to where I am.

AARON.   You will find the approach
And the means you want, I'm confident. Something
Will soon open a way to action.

RAMESES [*in the tent opening*].   Uncle.
I knew you as that. When I have thought of you
It has been as my uncle. You may not like it.
You may not want to see me, even.

MOSES. Welcome and unwelcome.

RAMESES.   I haven't come
From my father. I used schoolboy's worship, like myrrh
And cassia, to perpetuate you:
The immense and affable god in general's uniform,
Who came and went between wars, who filled the schoolroom;
And I could call him uncle. So when the memory
Broke its wrappings, and stood speaking like a man
On a noonday terrace, I decided to come nearer.

MOSES. Come on, then, and send the god to vanish finally
Into the lie that he always was.

RAMESES.   You spoke
To my father too suddenly.

MOSES.   Yes, we're precipitous,
We gods. We threw off the world, vegetable
And animal too, on the impulse of an imaginative
Moment. But we lost interest.

RAMESES.   You mean
I'm a boy to you still.

[31]

MOSES. You came by your boyhood honestly.
Mine I stole. I had no right to it.

AARON. Why
Do you turn him away, Moses? Why not talk to him?

MOSES. What would we talk of, Aaron? What quiet subject?
They tell me centuries of horror brood
In this vivid kingdom of fertile mud. Do you think
If we swung the rattle of conversation
Those centuries would fly off like so many crows?
They would wheel above us and come to feed again.

AARON. But where shall we find a better
Opportunity?

RAMESES. I have my father mapped
So that I know which way to travel. Listen,
Uncle—he says he would have recalled you, which means
He needs you here. He'll be friendly if you let him.
I kept a buckle of your uniform—this one, the lion-head.
Take it again, take our army and be our general.
You'll become inseparable from Egypt's safety;
Then he will listen. Then you can direct
His goodwill past yourself to these Israelites.

AARON. It's true. You have the buckle, and we're agreed, then.
My dreams were less; not a third as felicitous.

MOSES. Egypt and Israel both in me together!
How would that be managed? I should wolf
Myself to keep myself nourished. I could play
With wars, oh God, very pleasantly. You know
I prosper in a cloud of dust—you're wise
To offer me that. And Egypt would still be,
In spite of my fathers, a sufficient cause.

AARON. Yes, it would be sufficient.

[32]

MOSES.   Splendid, then.
What armour shall I wear? What ancestral metal
Above my heart? Rib, thighbone and skull:
Bones from the mines of Egypt. I will clank
To Egypt's victory in Israel's bones.
Does this please you? Does it not? Admire
How when preparing a campaign I become
Oblivious to day and night, and in
The action, obsessed. How will that do? I make
My future, put glory into Egypt, enjoy myself
Into your father's confidence—yes, that,
I know; and being there, perhaps I coax
Little concessions for the Hebrew cause
To justify me.—Idiot, idiot!
I should have lost them, Aaron, and be lost,
More than when in Midian I sat
Over my food and let them trudge in my bowels.

AARON. I have faith in your judgement. Nevertheless, this is
Something to be thought of, a reality of a kind.

MOSES. Like adultery.

MIRIAM.   Offer of a generalship?
Of course I don't understand. But like adultery?
To be a general? Do you mean us to think
You would refuse—

MOSES.   You both would like to see
Your brother fat, but your brother has a fancy
To be as lean as Israel.

RAMESES.   Will you promise to be patient?
There will be difficulties to be got over;
I have a father. But at some future time
When I am Pharaoh—

MOSES.   By then I may be free
To let my bones talk of their disinterest
In the world's affairs: and whether it is Hebrew
Or Egyptian, man will cry for me no longer.

MIRIAM. Listen!

AARON.   What is it?

MIRIAM.   Nothing, nothing—I imagined—
Why should he be back at this time? What
Could bring him now? Listen!

MOSES.   What do you hear?

MIRIAM. It's the call he gives when he's reaching home.

AARON.   Her son.
It's Shendi.

MIRIAM.   Something has happened.
Why is the palace here? What are you doing here
In my home? He cannot even come home.

RAMESES.   Is this
Egypt?

MIRIAM. Do you hear him again? No nearer, no nearer.
He is being prevented. Can I get to him
Without being seen? Stay where you are. No one
Must see me, no one.

                    [*She goes out. In a moment* AARON *follows her*

RAMESES.   You all think of me
As an enemy.

MOSES.   We're not enemies so much
As creatures of division. You and I,
Rameses, like money in a purse,
Ring together only to be spent
For different reasons.

[34]

There will be summers to come
Which need the throne and lotus: a world
Richer for an Egypt prosperous in wisdom
Which you will govern.

RAMESES.   Am I never to see you?

MOSES. No, it would be better, never. Stay with your own:
    A people without blame which still
    Faces the good future. My own purpose
    Would only bring you confusion. Forget me, Rameses.

RAMESES. That anyway is impossible. I know
    I bear your mark, and how will you obliterate
    That? Do you forget the feel of the year
    When you were as I am? They count me as a man,
    Just. But the boy is still in my head and mouth.
    I feel him there. I speak him. I should burn
    Throne and lotus gladly if I could break
    Myself of boyhood, if burning would do it. But you
    Are clear and risen roundly over the hazes.
    You have the formula. I need it.

MOSES.   Clear?
    Evidence of that! Where in this drouthy
    Overwatered world can you find me clarity?
    What spirit made the hawk? a bird obedient
    To grace, a bright lash on the cheek of the wind
    And drawn and ringed with feathered earth and sun,
    An achievement of eternity's birdsmith. But did he
    Also bleak the glittering charcoal of the eyes
    And sharpen beak and claws on his hone of lust?
    What language is life? Not one I know.
    A quarrel in God's nature. But you, at least,
    Are pronounceable: heir of Egypt, heir of Egypt.
    That is yourself.

RAMESES.   You mean I'm of no value
  Except to be Egypt's ornament.

MOSES.   Of much
  Value; infinite.

RAMESES.   But we stay unfriendly?

MOSES. Because I taste your boyhood and remember mine
  And like them both.

RAMESES.   But even so—

MOSES.   You shall stay as you are.

RAMESES. Exactly as I am, a friend of Moses.

MOSES. They're coming with Shendi. Keep with me in the shadow.

            Enter MIRIAM *and* AARON, *supporting* SHENDI

MIRIAM. He has been so strong. Are you ill? How are you ill?
  You can speak, surely you can speak? We don't know them;
  That's what is worst—our own—even in childhood
  They say so little.

AARON.   Lie here, Shendi.

MIRIAM.   Still
  And quiet. What shall I do for him?

AARON.   Give him this water.

MIRIAM. A sip, and then you shall have more.

SHENDI. They'll come.

MIRIAM.   Keep yourself quiet.

SHENDI.   Yes, they will come,
  They'll come for me, they'll find me!

AARON.   What have you done?

MIRIAM. Done?

                            [36]

SHENDI.   What are you holding me for? Must I always
  Be held? It was the sun! Don't you know that?
  They make madmen in the sun. Thousands of madmen
  Have been made in the sun. They say nothing, nothing at all,
  But suddenly they're running—no, not they,
  It's only their bodies that are running: the madmen
  Are still standing in the sun, watching their bodies
  Run away. Can they kill me for that? Or what, or what?
  It was the strike that started it!

AARON.   What have you said!
  What strike?

MIRIAM.   He's ill!

SHENDI.   No, it was the sun; not the strike,
  The sun. The noise of the strike, the whips.

AARON.   The strike?
  What was it? What do you mean?

SHENDI.   The spermy bastards!
  They make us hit the earth like spit.

MIRIAM.   What are you saying?
  Don't ask him any more!

AARON.   I'll make him tell me. What strike?
  What are you saying?

SHENDI.   I don't know what has happened.
  The brickmakers began it. A youngster was with me,
  Twelve years old, and he left me to watch the trouble.
  I saw them take him away, they dragged him off
  To the captain at the gate, because he was watching.
  It has nothing to do with it. It's the sun. Have you heard
  The order? They'll not give us straw to make the bricks;
  We must gather the straw ourselves; but the tale of bricks

Must be more, more! What does it matter? Who says
It matters? They're coming for me.

MIRIAM.   It cannot happen,
Shendi, it cannot.

MOSES.   Cannot happen, cannot be.
Cannot. Earth, life, ourselves are impossibility;
What is this Pharaoh who answers me with this?

SHENDI.   Who's that?
My uncle, is it? The great fellow that was.
The man who thought he was Egypt. Have you come
To try again, murderer? Look at your crop of relations
And how they do in the land you dunged for us.
Do you hear that? They're whipping the side of the tent.
You know I can't stand up, they've come for me,
You know it was the sun—uncle, uncle!

MIRIAM. It was neighbours talking, it was only the neighbours.
                                      —Aaron,
It was neighbours talking. Wasn't it, wasn't it?

Enter TWO OVERSEERS
                                   No, no!

1ST OVERSEER. Nice family. Here's the man we want.

2ND OVERSEER.   Get up,
Little rat. So you'd strike? We'll teach you striking.
Striking's our speciality. Eh? Not bad! We'll strike him!

MIRIAM. He's sick—can't you see?

1ST OVERSEER.   That's enough of that.

RAMESES.   What is this?
Weren't you told I had sent for him?

2ND OVERSEER.   My crimes!

RAMESES. Well, weren't you told?

1ST OVERSEER. No, sir; no, your holiness; not told.
I beg your pardon, sir. I didn't see you, my lord, didn't see you.

RAMESES. I tell you now. I sent for him. Go away.

1ST OVERSEER. Yes, lord.

2ND OVERSEER. Yes, almighty.

[*They back away out of sight*

MIRIAM. You're here, Shendi, you're here. The prince has kept
you.
He spoke for you.

SHENDI. No one warned—What are you doing with me?
Is it a trick? What did I say before they came?
My lord forgive me, I was ill.

RAMESES. Nothing will hurt you. You can rest.
You have seen enough of Egypt in this tent.

[*Exit* RAMESES

AARON. I begin to have hope.
Eh, Moses? This is the boy who will be our man,
The palace key. In the belly of our misfortune
We find our hope.

MOSES. We're not concerned with hope,
Or with despair; our need is something different:
To confront ourselves, to create within ourselves
Existence which cannot fail to be fulfilled.
It will not be through this boy, nor through
Thankless palace manœuvring and compromise.

AARON. Where will you turn, then?

MOSES. Where shall I look for triumph?
Somewhere, not beyond our scope, is a power
Participating but unharnessed, waiting
To be led towards us. Good has a singular strength

[39]

Not known to evil; and I, an ambitious heart
Needing interpretation. But not through Rameses,
Never through Rameses. I will not use him!

CURTAIN

SCENE THREE

A room in the Palace, giving on to the terrace of Scene One. ANATH *is standing on the terrace.* TEUSRET'S *voice is heard calling 'Rameses! Rameses!' It draws nearer.* ANATH *comes into the room and listens for* TEUSRET'S *voice which now comes from farther away. She turns to go back to the terrace. Enter* RAMESES.

ANATH. Have you seen your father?

RAMESES. He has made me a present of my future
   With the royal seal attached. I'm to marry
   The King of Syria's daughter. Did you know?

ANATH. He told me he would ask this of you.

RAMESES. When I woke this morning I thought nothing of the
        future,
   Only of today, and what I remembered of the past.
   And yet in these twelve hours the future
   Has suddenly come up, two-legged, huge, as though to say
   'See nothing but me.' First Moses, with his fixed purpose
   Walking ahead of us, as absolute
   As a man's death. And now this other future,
   A stranger from Syria to be the focus
   Of my life, my senses and devotion, if it may be.

ANATH. I wish you happiness.

RAMESES.   Where is Teusret?

ANATH.   Everywhere.
Put your hand in one place, she is already
Beating her wings in another.

RAMESES.   Listen—look—
What is this 'now', the moment we're now crossing?
Can this truth vanish?
Look, your shadow thrown over the chair,
That dog's jerking bark, the distance of whistling,
A gate clanging-to, the water thrown into the yard,
Your fingers travelling your bracelet, my voice—listen,
My voice—your breathing—

[TEUSRET *is heard calling* RAMESES

                And Teusret running through the empty rooms.
It is true for us now, but not till now, and never
To be again. I want it for myself.
This is my life.

Enter TEUSRET

                It has gone.

TEUSRET.   I've found you at last.
Where have you been hidden? Where were you?

RAMESES.   With father.

TEUSRET. For an hour!
No one could tell me. The rooms were all deserted.
Just as it happens in my sleep sometimes; but then
The door on the other side of the room is always
Closing behind you, and the room is empty—I never
Come to you.

RAMESES.   But, awake, it's different. You find me.

TEUSRET. Why did he talk for so long?

[41]

RAMESES.   I'm to be married
He says.

TEUSRET. I had a riddle to ask you. Fareti
Taught it to me.

RAMESES.   What is it?

TEUSRET.   Rameses,
When will you be married?

RAMESES.   Soon, he says.

TEUSRET. Why? Why? You can't! What does he mean?
Then—if you did—Why have you said so? Oh,
Why did you say it?

RAMESES.   Teusret—

TEUSRET.   Who is it?

RAMESES.   The Syrian.
Her name is Phipa.

TEUSRET.   Do you think that's pretty?
Phipa, Phipa, Phipa! The noise a flute makes
When the mouth's too full of saliva. You won't do it.

RAMESES. What can I say?

ANATH.   Teusret, we all, you will find,
Belong to Egypt: our lives go on the loom
And our land weaves. And the gods know we need
Some such alliance. If the dynasty is safe
We can at least be partly ourselves. He will need
Both of us still.

TEUSRET.   He won't. He will be changed.
The days will be different and I shall be the same.
How shall I be happy then?

Enter SETI

[42]

                              Will *you* be?
Are you glad?

SETI.   Can you imagine, Teusret,
   The frantic compulsion which first fetched man forming
   And breathing out of the earth's dust? Such
   A compulsion of beauty has this Phipa of Syria,
   With the addition of wit and a good head for business.
   She's immensely rich. Homegoing sailors,
   When there are no stars, steer perfectly for Syria
   Merely by thinking of her. So they say.
   A figure of her, hung under the stern
   And kissing the wake, ensures a harvest of fish.

TEUSRET. What a tale!

SETI.   Well, yes, but she has beauty.

TEUSRET.   Flowers for Rameses
   Then! We must make it an occasion. I'll fetch my lute
   And celebrate. Garlands! I'll make you into
   A nice little afternoon god. Don't go away.

RAMESES. Here, Teusret—

TEUSRET.   You have earned a ceremony.
   Would you rather have me in tears? This isn't silliness
   But a proper formality. I need to do it.
   Wait, all of you.   [*Exit* TEUSRET

ANATH.   Let her do what she must.

RAMESES.   Father,
   I have something to ask you. It has to do with Moses.

SETI. He needn't trouble you.

RAMESES.   Nor any of us. But haven't you
   Overlooked his nephew?

                              [43]

SETI. This is nothing to you.
Nothing to you at all.

RAMESES. Nothing at all.
Moses has a sister and a nephew.
The nephew's a labourer. Might there not here be a way
By which you could come at Moses?

SETI. Statesmanship,
My son, is the gods' gift to restrain their own
Infidelities to man. As for Moses,
I'll comprehend him when he's comprehensible.

RAMESES. Such as a commission for this nephew; or a place in the
palace.
What do you say? Can you talk of honours
To a man whose family is unhonoured? I don't know,
But you will know.

SETI. Who told you to speak of him?
What do you know of this name that you're bandying? Anath?
Is this your influence?

ANATH. Am I a planet,
To be so influential? No, Seti, it is not.
I would rather infect him with something less dubious
Than the blood of Moses.

Enter TEUSRET *with a lute and flowers*

TEUSRET. Look, I have them. I got them
Out of my room. They were round my bronze Isis.
Shall I have offended her?

SETI. Do you know this nephew?

ANATH. I've seen him.

SETI. How did he promise?

[44]

ANATH.   He promised to be male,
  As though he might have the ability for a beard
  I thought.

TEUSRET. Are you all ready for the ceremony?
  Rameses, you must be in a chair; this chair.

RAMESES. Can it be tried?

SETI.   What is it now?

RAMESES.   To mark
  My coming of age. May I commission the nephew?

SETI. That is still to be known. I must have precise
  Information of him. Now forget the question.

TEUSRET. Why must you go
  Before you see Rameses in flowers? And when
  Have you ever heard me play on my lute?   [*Exit* SETI
                          Has no one
  Told him he has a daughter?

ANATH.   The flowers were schooled
  With salamanders, to be so enduring
  In this furnace.

RAMESES.   Will he really do it?

ANATH.   The land
  Is rocking, remember. He'll take hold even of grass.

TEUSRET. Let me begin. Neither of you has any sense
  Of occasion. These on your shoulders. What *are* flowers?
  What is the bridge to be crossed, I wonder,
  From a petal to being a wing or a hand? These
  For your brows. Does the scent of them sicken you?
  My pollen fingers.

RAMESES.   They're shattering already.

[45]

TEUSRET. Some of them are too full.

RAMESES. You've brought me the garden.
Here's an earwig on my hand.

TEUSRET. Tread on it. Now
You're ripe to receive a god. Isn't he, Aunt?
Does he look noble? My brother in bloom.

RAMESES [*treading on the earwig*]. Out goes he. Let's get your singing over.

TEUSRET [*staring*]. I have to remember you. Sing with me.

ANATH. I?
Sing? With the crack in my voice? Not songs for bridegrooms.
Only songs in the minor, where a false note
Can be taken to be excessive sensibility.

TEUSRET. Nothing, nothing will go on in the old way.
I wonder, can I remember which is the key? [*She touches the lute*

RAMESES. Did you know my father had ordered the Israelites
To gather their own straw?

ANATH. Yes, I knew.

RAMESES. Why did he?

ANATH. A little show of invulnerability.

RAMESES. Is Moses safe here?

TEUSRET. I wish there were echoes in this room,
A choir of them, to be company for my voice.
You will have to help me when I lose myself.
[*Sings*] Why should there be two
Where one will do,
Step over this shadow and tell me
And my heart will make a ring
Sighing in a circle

And my hands will beckon and bring
The maiden fortune who befell me
O fortune, fortune.

Enter SETI

You see, father,—doesn't he look married already?

[*Sings*] Why do we breathe and wait
So separate?
The whirl in the shell and the sand
Is time going home to time
Kissing to a darkness.
So shall we go, so shall we seem
In the gardens, hand in hand.
O fortune, fortune.
So changed against the sun—

[*She is interrupted by* MOSES, *who enters bearing in his arms
a dead Israelite boy*

ANATH. What are we to have now?

SETI. What is this? Isn't it enough that you broke
Into Egypt unasked but you must—

MOSES.   This is your property.
Of little value. Shall I bury it in your garden?
You need have no anxiety. It will not grow.

ANATH. Oh, in the name of the gods—

SETI.   Is your reason gone?

MOSES [*laying the body at* SETI'S *feet*]. Look: worthless, worthless.
The music needn't stop.
You killed him.

SETI.   As I thought; you've let your brain
Suffer in this heat. I saw, in the first few words
You spoke this morning, it would end in this.

[47]

TEUSRET. Rameses! That boy!

RAMESES.   That isn't death
  Lying on the ground.

TEUSRET.   It is! It is! It is!

SETI. Well? Tell me: is it an act of sanity
  To carry this child here? I'm sorry to see it.
  Take him and have him buried. You know it wasn't
  Done by me.

MOSES.   It was done of you. You'll not
  Escape from yourself through the narrows between By and Of.
  Your captain killed him on the metal of your gates, as with
  A score of others. If it wasn't done of you
  Fetch the captain, condemn him to death, and watch
  How he'll stare.

SETI.   I'll see the man. It 's understood.

MOSES. Who understands? And what is understood?
  If you move your foot only a little forward
  Your toe will be against your power. Is this
  How you imagined your strength to be—ungrowing,
  Unbreathing, a child, and dead? Out of him
  Comes your army, your fleet, the cliff of gold
  You move on, pride, place, adulation
  And name. Fetch in your captain,
  Fetch in your thousand captains, and condemn them
  For the murder of your power.

SETI.   Nature is lavish,
  And in return for being understood,
  Not hoarded, gives us civilization.
  Would you have the earth never see purple
  Because the murex dies? Blame, dear Moses,

[48]

The gods for their creative plan which is
Not to count the cost but enormously
To bring about.

MOSES.   And so they bring about
The enormity of Egypt. Is that the full
Ambition of your gods? Egypt is only
One golden eruption of time, one flying spark
Attempting the ultimate fire. But who can say
What secrets my race has, what unworked seams
Of consciousness in mind and soul? Deny
Life to itself and life will harness and ride you
To its purpose. My people shall become themselves,
By reason of their own god who speaks within them.
What I ask is that I may lead them peaceably
Into the wilderness for a space, to find
Their god and so become living men at last.

SETI. More favours, something new. What god is this?

MOSES. The inimitable patience who doesn't yet
Strike you down.

SETI.   He and I have something in common
If he has patience. My trust is Egypt
And the maturity of the world.

MOSES. You know well enough invasion is probable,
Unrest is in and out of doors, your southern half
Splits from the north, the lords at your table
Are looking down at their hands. And flowing through all
Is the misery of my blood. Let that be clean
First, and then your flesh may heal.

SETI.   Enough,
I have nursed you enough. Now dungeons can nurse you.
Your god can find you behind the walls
And return your reason when he will.

[49]

ANATH. Seti! Are you sure? Will the surly half
Of Egypt believe he was mad?

SETI.   Do you still play
At being his mother?

ANATH.   Do you think I do?

RAMESES. There could have been some other way than this.
Is only Israel present to you,
As once it was only Egypt?
Are you still Moses? Or who? Who are you?

ANATH. Does he know?

SETI.   A man without laws.

MOSES. What are the laws? Tell me, you taker of lives!
I am here by fury and the heart. Is that not
A law? I am here to appease the unconsummated
Resourceless dead, to join life to the living.
Is that not underwritten by nature? Is that
Not a law? Do not ask me why I do it!
I live. I do this thing. I was born this action.
Despite you, through you, upon you,
I am compelled.

> [*A distant long cracking sound of thunder.* MOSES *jerks back
> his head to listen*

                        Are we overheard? Behind
The door that shuts us into life, there is
An ear. Am I given the power
To do what I am?
What says the infinite eavesdropper?

> [*From horizon to horizon the sky is beaten into thunder*

CURTAIN TO ACT ONE

[50]

ACT TWO

SCENE ONE

MIRIAM'S *tent, the evening of the same day.* MOSES. AARON.

MOSES. Look: I shall divide them
Into groups a hundred or a hundred and fifty strong,
Each with a man to lead them, one they can trust,
Such as this man you mention, Morshad—
And the man I spoke with this evening. Put them down.

AARON. Morshad and Zedeth. Yes, I have them.

MOSES. And then
This morning's rioting, the man who started that,
Whatever his name is. Will they listen to him again?

[AARON *goes to the tent-opening and looks out*

He made his move too early, some few days
Too soon.

AARON. I thought I felt the earth quiver.

MOSES. What is he called?

AARON. The earth has moved. It stirred
Like an animal. Moses!

MOSES. The man has a name. Put him down.

AARON. Something unnatural has come awake
Which should have slept until time was finished.
Listen! Did you hear a roar? A building
Has collapsed. The dust is like a cloud, higher
Than the city. Will you see?

[51]

MOSES.   We have something more to do
Than to listen to falling cities. The dust will settle
While we Hebrews die. Come on; give me the names.

AARON. Why does this mean nothing to you?
Why won't you come and see it?

MOSES.   The names, the names.

[MIRIAM *stands in the opening, with a pitcher*

MIRIAM. All the water is blood.

AARON.   Miriam! What is happening to the city?

MIRIAM. There's no water, no water. Nothing but blood.

AARON. Then my fear has foundation. The sun has set
On truth altogether. The evening's a perjury!
Let none of us be duped by it.

MIRIAM.   The water
Is blood. The river floods it over the fields.
The wells stink of it.

AARON.   What are you saying?

MIRIAM.   Go out then
And see it yourself. The men who were thirsty enough
To drink what came, are lying at the well-heads
Vomiting.

MOSES.   What men? Ours?

MIRIAM.   Egyptians.

MOSES.   Miriam,
What have you there?

MIRIAM.   I filled my pitcher. We all
Filled our pitchers, everyone, in spite of—

[52]

Do you think it could happen to us? To them
Perhaps, something might happen; to the others but not
To ourselves.

MOSES [*bringing his hand out of the pitcher*]. Not to ourselves. To
the others.

MIRIAM.   Your hand
Has water on it! It is water!

MOSES.   From which well
Was this drawn?

MIRIAM.   Our own. Are we likely to use the Egyptians'?
But I saw it, we all saw it.

MOSES.   The sun this last hour
Has been that colour. Doesn't it at evening
Fall directly on our well?

MIRIAM.   The sun? Are we
Talking about the sun? Tell me I'm lying
And look at my feet. We slopped in blood flooding
From the Nile. I saw the Egyptians who drank it.

MOSES.   The Nile.
The Egyptians! But this water came from our well
Not theirs.—Was I waiting, Aaron? I was waiting
Without expectation. But surely, I already knew?
We with our five bare fingers
Have caused the strings of God to sound.
Creation's mutehead is dissolving, Aaron.
Our lives are being lived into our lives.
We are known!

MIRIAM.   Do you think it was you who made the Egyptians
Vomit? We may as well all be mad.
Where is Shendi?

[53]

AARON. What's this?
Isn't there confusion enough? Confusion I call it!
A contradiction of what we have always known
To be conclusive: an ugly and impossible
Mistake in nature. And you, you of all men
Accept it, identify yourself with it. It must be
Denied. What has become of you since yesterday?
Is it not possible still to be plain men
Dealing with a plain situation? Must we see
Visions? You were an unchallengeable leader once.
That is the man I follow. A plain soldier.

MIRIAM. Where can Shendi be?

MOSES. The plainest soldier is sworn to the service of riddles.
Our strategy is written on strange eternal paper.
We may decide to advance this way or that way
But we are lifted forward by a wind
And when it drops we see no more of the world.
Shall we live in mystery and yet
Conduct ourselves as though everything were known?
If, in battle upon the sea, we fought
As though on land, we should be more embroiled
With water than the enemy. Are we on sea
Or land, would you say?

AARON. Sea? Land? For pity's sake
Stay with reality.

MOSES. If I can penetrate
So far.

MIRIAM. Why hasn't Shendi come home yet? It's past his time.
He should have stayed here the rest of the day.
Will you let me out of this intolerable night?
Are we going to stand here for ever?

[54]

SHENDI [*in the tent-opening*].   Mother!

MIRIAM.   Shendi,
  Has nothing happened to you? Let me see you and be
  Reassured. Were you harmed by what I saw?

SHENDI. What have you seen? Nothing happened? Everything!
  We've stepped across to a new life. Where were we living?
  It was the appearance, of course, the appearance of hell.
  Nothing like it at all, except in our minds, our poor
  Minds. I was going to make you try to guess,
  But such an idea could never come at a guess.
  They've made me an officer!

MIRIAM. I don't—understand what you mean.

SHENDI.   Your son! You see?
  They've made him an officer. Like an Egyptian officer.
  Like? I am one. We didn't know, that was all,
  The world is perfectly fair, something to laugh at.
  The ridiculous difference between me this morning
  And now! They found I was better with head than hands.

MIRIAM. Shendi, did you come by way of the wells? Did you see
    them?

SHENDI. I expect so. They say they're diseased. Can you imagine
  How I felt when they took me by the arm and led me
  Apart from the other men? I almost fought them.
  I knew I was going to be beaten—

MIRIAM.   Shendi, stop!
  What are you saying?

SHENDI.   Hell is done, done,
  Done with, over!

MOSES.   For you.

[55]

MIRIAM.   They would never do it.
But then tonight everything is to be believed.
Nothing has any truth and anything is true.

SHENDI. I report at the officers' quarters
In half an hour. I'll take some of my things
Along with me now. Has the world always been known
To spring such wonders, do you think? You're to live with me,
Mother, do you understand? Follow on later
And ask for the new officer. At the officers' quarters.
Have you something you can give me to wrap this linen in?
The Libyans have broken across the border and massacred
Two companies of the border regiment.

AARON.   What?
A massacre? When was this?

SHENDI.   I don't know when.
Where have you put my razor? Four hundred Egyptians
Killed, they say. They talked as though
I were already one of themselves. They say
There's also a rumour of revolution in the south.

AARON. Moses, do you hear?

SHENDI.   Where is my razor?

MIRIAM.   There.
Did you see the wells? I don't know what life's doing.
I don't know how we're to think.

AARON.   Ambitiously.
These incidents all march our way. The Libyans
Over the border—revolution—Time
Is preparing for us with a timely unrest.
We came to Egypt at the perfect hour as it happens.

SHENDI. That's enough of talk like that!

[56]

MIRIAM.   As it happens;
  If we knew what happens. Shendi an officer!
  Will this be what we want, at last? As the Nile
  Happens into blood. Shendi an officer.

SHENDI. And the officers' quarters, remember: comfort.

MIRIAM.   As massacre
  And revolution happens. As tomorrow
  Happens, whatever happens tomorrow.

SHENDI.   Come on,
  I must go.

MOSES.   Refuse this commission.

SHENDI.   What did you say?

MOSES. Refuse this commission.

MIRIAM.   Refuse it?

SHENDI.   Listen to that!
  As my uncle happens, this is no surprise.
  Only one of the family must rise
  And glow in Egypt. The rest of us can keep
  Against the ground, and lose the whole damned world
  Because Moses prefers it. But in spite of that,
  In spite of that, generous brother of my mother,
  We hope to live a little.

AARON.   As who does not?
  The Pharaoh, I quite see, will have his motives.
  But we can outmove motives to our advantage;
  And here surely is a kind of proffered hand.

MIRIAM. Why should he refuse? How could he refuse?

SHENDI.   It's clear
  Why he says it. It was he who came back for recognition
  And I have got it.

[57]

MOSES.   Make yourself live, then, Shendi;
But be sure it is life. The golden bear Success
Hugs a man close to its heart; and breaks his bones.
What have they said, these Egyptians?
Come with us and we'll treat you well.
Not, come with us and we will treat
You and your people well.

AARON.   They will come in time
Even to say that.

SHENDI [*to* MOSES]. This sounds well
Indeed, from you!

MIRIAM.   Shendi is to be all
That he can become—all; and I say so,
I who made him. Am I to go on holding
The guilt for his unhappiness when opportunity
Offers to deliver me from it? Guilt it was,
And damnation, for giving him birth. This will let me loose!

SHENDI. Why do we listen to him? I know how to value
The first fairness I've known. If you think so little
Of being alive, uncle, you will find they're assembling
Spears to flash on Libya. Why not make something
Of that? The tradition is that, once upon a time,
You didn't know the meaning of apprehension
Or fear—back in those days when it was you
They treated well.

ANATH [*in the tent-opening*]. Does he still not apprehend
Or fear?

SHENDI. Madam, madam—

ANATH.   What are you doing
To Egypt, Moses?

MOSES.   What have you come for?

[58]

ANATH.   You.
   What are you doing to Egypt, Moses?

MOSES.   What
   Is Egypt doing to Egypt?

ANATH.   Or Egypt to you.
   Come with me. I came by the old walks.
   What have I seen? You shall come with me
   And see it and tell me, and see the men and women
   Bewildered in the doorways, for the name of their world
   Has changed from home to horror. And is this
   What you have in your heart for Egypt? Then favour me
   And also have it in your eyes.

MOSES.   But why
   Do you come to me? To whose blood has the Nile
   Turned? It isn't mine. Can it be the spilt blood
   Of Israelites that is flowing back on Egypt?
   Why come to me?

ANATH.   He wants reason! Rationalize
   The full moon and the howling dog. I have less
   Inclination to be here than the dog has to howl.
   If you come with me to Seti, he's ready to talk to you.

MOSES. We've talked already.

ANATH.   He'll let you take your Hebrews
   To make their worship, or whatever you want of them,
   On some conditions which he'll tell you.

AARON.   Good.
   Events are moving.

MOSES.   If Seti is so ready,
   Why did you make the walk through the ominous evening
   To remind me that I'm in Egypt?

[59]

ANATH.   Because he is sitting
Pressing his thumbs together, wedged inactive
In between his decision and pride. What it is
To have to do with men! They live too large.
I'm ready to take you.

MOSES. I'll go.

AARON.   This will be a great day for Israel.

MIRIAM. My son has been made an officer.

ANATH.   I shall be glad
Not to be alone this time, with the earth
Wavering to a hint of doom. I suppose
There have to be powers of darkness, but they should keep
To the rules. The sky is lighter. The worst may be over.

MOSES. Aaron, you will come too.

AARON.   It has been easier
Than I should have thought possible this morning.

                    [*Exeunt* ANATH, MOSES, *and* AARON

SHENDI. What is this business the Pharaoh has with my uncle?

MIRIAM. I mustn't think of Moses. Many things
I must be sure to keep my thoughts quite away from.
What is it we have to do? A dark mind
And he has followed that woman.

SHENDI. Will he try to stop my commission going through?

MIRIAM. No, no, he's forgotten it.

SHENDI.   What does he matter, then?
I'm an officer!

MIRIAM.   How could the water be blood, Shendi?

SHENDI. What?

                    [60]

MIRIAM.   I'll put your things together for you.
How grand we shall be!

CURTAIN

SCENE TWO

A room in the Palace.   SETI.   ANATH.

ANATH. Keep the window covered, Seti. The terrace
Crackles with dying locusts. I looked out.
I seemed to look within, on to myself,
When I stood there and looked out over Egypt.
The face of all this land is turned to the wall.
I looked out, and when I looked to the north I saw
Instead of quiet cattle, glutted jackals,
Not trees and pasture but vulture-bearing boughs
And fields which had been sown with hail. And looking
To the south I saw, like falling ashes after fire,
Death after thirst, death after hunger, death
After disease. And when I looked to the east
I saw an old woman ridding herself of lice;
And to the west, a man who had no meaning
Pushing thigh-deep through drifts of locusts.

SETI. Well; these things are finished.

ANATH.   And what happens
Now? What will you do when the mourners have done
Wailing, and men look across the havoc of their fields
And the bones of their cattle and say: You did this,
What happens now?

[61]

SETI.   Why am I to be blamed
For all the elemental poisons that come up fungoid
Out of the damps and shadows which our existence
Moves in? Can I put peace into the furious
God-epilepsy of earthquake and eruption?
What am I but one of those you pity?

ANATH. You tricked him, you tricked Moses, and not once
But seven times. First when I, against
All my self-warning, approached the unapproachable
And brought him to you. Didn't you make him promises
Then, and break them? And that night your promises
Plagued our ears with a croaking mockery,
With an unceasing frog-echo of those words
Which had meant nothing; with a plague of frogs!
A second time you made promises, and a third time
And a fourth: seven times you've broken them
While the stews of creation had their way with Egypt.

SETI. You say this, concoct this legend; you have become
Infected with the venom that's against me.

ANATH. No, I've no venom. I've no more efficacy
Than a fishwife who has been made to breed against
Her will; and so I'm shrill and desperate.
No power against misery! That's what our lives add up to.
Our spacious affability, our subtle intelligence,
Our delicate consciousness of worlds beyond the world,
Our persuasive dignity when sacrificing to the gods,
Our bodies and our brains can all become
Slutted with lice between afternoon and evening.
You tricked him a second time, and that is what
You saw: sweet made foul. And then the third time
And we became the dungheap, the lusted of flies,
The desirable excretion. Our pleasantness was flyblown.

SETI. I've suffered this once with Egypt—

ANATH.   You tricked Moses.
And what has come of it I would bring back to you
Until pity came out of you like blood to the knife,
Remembering how disease swept all the cattle,
How we could not sleep for intolerable lowing
Till daylight rounded up the herds of wolftorn
Death. You tricked him, and that feculent moment
Filthied our blood and made of us a nation
Loathsome with boils. You had stirred up the muck
Which the sweet gods thought fit to make us of
When they first formed man, the primal putrescence
We keep hidden under our thin dress of health.
What a pretty world, this world of filthmade kings!
When, after the sixth time, the hail came down,
I laughed. The hail was hard, metallic, cold
And clean, beating on us with the ferocity
Of brainbright anger. As cut diamonds, clean,
Clean, and fit to be beaten down by. When
It stamped out the gardens and cracked the skulls of birds
It bruised away the memory of vermin
And struck our faces fairly. If then, if only
Then our consciousness had gone clean out,
Or if then you had let these Israelites go with Moses,
We should not now so vainly
Shuffle our fingers in the dust to find
The name we once were known by. But you tricked
For the seventh time, and then the curse of the locusts
Strangled the whole air, the whole earth,
Devoured the last leaf of the old life
That we had sometime lived. The land is naked
To the bone, and men are naked beyond the bone,

Down to the barest nakedness which until now
Hope kept covered up. Now climb and sit
On the throne of this reality, and be
A king.

SETI.   Anath! These plagues were not my doing
And you know they were not. No man would say I caused them.
Only a woman with her mind hung
With a curtain of superstition would say so.

ANATH.   I admit it.
I am superstitious. I have my terrors.
We are born too inexplicably out
Of one night's pleasure, and have too little security:
No more than a beating heart to keep us probable.
There must be other probabilities.
You tricked Moses after I had gone myself
To bring him to you, and what followed followed.

SETI. It is true I made certain concessions to Moses
And reconsidered them. I was prepared
To let him have his way, if in return
He would use his great abilities to our advantage.
But am I to have no kind of surety
That he'll return, after this godhunt of his?
I said to him Take the men but their wives and children
Must remain. And then I went further: I told him to take
Both men and women, but the children must stay. And at last
I only insisted on their cattle, since our cattle
Were dead. I'll not be panicked by this chain
Of black coincidence, which he with his genius
For generalship has taken advantage of.
He presumes upon the eternal because he has
No power to strike his bargain. I have not done
These things to Egypt. I'll not hear it be said.

ANATH. Well, they're done. Blame has no value anyway.
There's not one of us whose life doesn't make mischief
Somewhere. Now after all you've had to give in.
At last, this morning, he has carried the day.
We must calculate again, calculate without Moses.
I picked unhappy days in those girlhood rushes.
But at least we can sweep away the locusts.

SETI. How carried the day? It is he
Who must calculate again. You understand
There will be no postponement of Rameses' marriage;
We can look forward to that, and the happy outcome
Of my careful policy.

ANATH.   What do you mean?
Moses by now has called the assembly of the Hebrews.
By now Egypt has heard the news. Moses
Has taken policy out of your hands.

SETI.   I sent
Word after him.

ANATH.   Seti! What word did you send?
What have you done?

SETI.   I have only been careful
To protect your future. Even before Moses
Had gone three steps from the palace there came the news
Of another defeat. Fate has taken a hammer
To chip and chip at our confidence.
But while I still have Moses to come at my call
I have not lost him. And while he needs my help
He will continue to come. And when he is tired—
We'll make a bargain.

[65]

ANATH.   All this, then, over again.
You're mad. It isn't we who make the bargains
In this life, but chance and time. I tell you it's madness!

Enter RAMESES

RAMESES. Father,
Is it true you've withdrawn your latest promise to Moses?

SETI. Whatever I have done or not done isn't to be said
In a sentence.

RAMESES.   They say it's true. Wherever I have gone
Dank rumour has been rising off the pavements, chilling
Into the heart of the people: 'Pharaoh has refused
Moses again. What new disastrous day
Is coming?' I tell you I've been out walking
Under the burning windows of the people's eyes.
You've stood fast long enough. Let Moses take
The Hebrews.

SETI.   So you also are afraid of magic
And believe that this tall Moses can make a business
Out of curses? Do you suppose if I surrendered to him
There would be any less roaring in the wind
Or less infection in disease? Why
Aren't you beside me like another man,
Instead of so fretting me with nursery behaviour
That I could strike you? I made life in your mother
To hand me strength when I should need it. That life
Was you. I made you exactly for this time
And I find you screeching to escape it.

RAMESES.   I have been
Through streets that no men should have to walk in.
You must let the Hebrews go. Father, you must!

SETI. You know nothing, you little fool, nothing! Govern
By your idiocy when I am dead.

[66]

RAMESES. What
Will you leave for me to govern, or what by then
Shall I have become, what figure of faded purple
Who clears his throat on an unimportant throne?
I am to you only the boy who comes
To the door to say goodnight on his way to bed.
It's you who invite the future but it's I
Who have to entertain it, remember that.
What is expedience for you may become
Dark experience for me. And these last weeks
I've heard the future's loping footfall, as plague
Came after plague, and I knew the steps
Were not passing but approaching. You
Were persuading them. They came each time a little
Nearer, and each time closer to me.
Keep your word to Moses. Let him take them.

SETI. I tell you it isn't possible.

RAMESES. Then get
Yourself another heir, and make him eat
Your black bread of policy. Marry yourself
To this girl from Syria. My plans are different.

SETI. Your plans are different! You insolent cub, you spoiled
Insolent cub! And so your plans are different?
You've already made your plans!

RAMESES. Wait. What
Was that noise?

ANATH. The old familiar. A man crying out.
What difference is one man's groaning more or less?

RAMESES [*looking from the terrace*]. Oh horrible! What is it that
makes men
And makes them like this man? Abortions of nature.
It is true what they said.

[67]

ANATH.   What is true?

RAMESES. What the other officers said, what I thought they spread
     About out of malice: that Shendi outstruts them all,
     Drives the Hebrews harder than any Egyptian
     Drives them, hits them down with a readier fist,
     And smiles and thrives under the admiration
     Of the overseers. Go out on the terrace if you doubt me
     And see him, Shendi, the son of Miriam, a Jew
     Beating a Jew.

SETI.   So perhaps at last,
     So perhaps at last you will have seen
     That what you thought was child's play, black and white,
     Is a problem of many sides. And you will kindly
     Wait and learn. This fellow does the work
     Which you yourself suggested he should do
     And does it conscientiously, without sentiment.

RAMESES. I suggested he should do it. Yes.
     I put the whip in his hand. I raised that arm.
     I struck that Jew. I did it. I did not know
     How the things we do, take their own life after
     They are done, how they can twist themselves
     Into foul shapes. I can now see better
     The deathly ground we live on. Yes, all right,
     I have surrendered. Whatever happens will happen
     Without me. I've finished meddling.

ANATH.   Rameses!
     Of all the Jews one Jew has done this.

RAMESES.   It might be
     A thousand instead of one.

ANATH.   Rameses, only
     One Jew!

SETI. Would you even encourage the traitor
In my son, because of your fear of this Moses?

ANATH.   Yes,
I would make him rebellious, and if I could I would make
Every limb of your body rebellious;
I'd paralyse that pride which sends us packing
Into a daily purgatory of apprehension.

SETI. Turn yourselves all against me.
I stand now living and breathing only to protect
This country from disintegration.

ANATH.   Oh
The gods, how we fumble between right and wrong,
Between our salvation and our overthrow,
Like drunk men with a key in the dark who stand
At the right door but cannot get out of the cold.
May the moment of accident bless us.

RAMESES.   I shall not
Rebel again. That will be one trouble less.

SETI. Stand beside me. We're almost of equal height
And may yet come to be of equal mind;
And if that is so, one of us will find
The way of escape out of this distress
Of ours, either you or I.

                Enter KEF, *a Minister to the Pharaoh*

KEF.   My lord Pharaoh.

SETI. News; come on.

KEF.   Better to hear it alone.

SETI. Bad news. Well, let's have it. Catastrophe
Is no longer my secret. Let us have it all.

[69]

KEF. My lord—

SETI.   Go on, go on.

KEF.   A report that the Libyans
Have annihilated the reinforcing fifth
Division.

SETI.   It is impossible.

KEF.   They were surrounded
And surprised. Only six men got through.

SETI.   Six men.

RAMESES. Six men.

SETI.   They load me to the last inch.

Enter TEUSRET

TEUSRET.   Moses has come
Again. I saw him walking like a lion
Behind bars, up and down in your battered garden,
Rameses. The sentries had tried to hold him
But he broke through their spears as though he didn't see them.
He looked at me, his eyes the colour of anger;
He looked at me and gripped a mulberry-bough
And broke it, and said Go to your father, fetch me
Your father.

SETI.   He can walk longer and break more boughs.
He shall wait, and find that Egypt is hard ground
Under his lion's walk. [*To* KEF] Go out to the overseers
And tell them to tighten discipline, to give
No rest to those Hebrews, not to let man, woman
Or child straighten their backs while they still stand.
I shall not see him until I choose; and, when
I choose, for his people's sake, he'll do what I need.
See this done.

[70]

ANATH. Seti, take care; take care
What you do.

SETI. Let Moses think again what behaviour
Is best, best to save his people. [*Exit*

TEUSRET. Rameses,
What is it? Why are you so silent? Are you afraid
As well? Are you afraid? Are you, Rameses?

RAMESES. Why should I be? The sweet part of the world's
All over, but that's nothing. It had to go.
My mind had lutes and harps and nodding musicians
Who drowned my days with their casual tunes. They have been
Paid off by this honest hour. And now I hear
My voice raised in deathly quiet. It's insufferable
That my voice, without the accompaniment of good fortune,
Should be so out of key, so faltering,
So cracking with puberty.—Aunt Anath,
What's the meaning of my manhood, to be found
So helpless, to be so helpless: what is there to do
Which I could do and haven't yet seen?

ANATH. We're no longer alone.

[MOSES *stands in the doorway*

TEUSRET. Look, Rameses.

MOSES. Where is Seti?

ANATH. He will not see you.

MOSES. When will he learn? When,
When, when will he learn? We have agonized
This land with anger for too many days.

ANATH. You
And he together. No birth is worth this labour.

[71]

MOSES. For three hundred years the pangs of this coming deliver-
    ance
    Have been suffered by my people, while Egypt played.
    But now Egypt suffers, and she says
    This is a new hell. But hell is old;
    And you yourself sitting in sunlight
    Embroidered on it with your needle. Hell
    Is old, but until now
    It fed on other women, that is all.

ANATH. And all is the innocent as well as the guilty;
    All is the small farmer and the singing fisherman
    And the wife who sweeps; tomorrow's boy as well
    As yesterday's. All these, while Seti twists
    To have his way, must go to your fire like sticks.

RAMESES [looking from the terrace]. The gods help them now! The
    gods help those Hebrews!

MOSES. It must be one people or another, your people
    Or mine. You appeal to Moses,
    But Moses is now only a name and an obedience.
    It is the God of the Hebrews, a vigour moving
    In a great shadow, who draws the bow
    Of his mystery, to loose this punishing arrow
    Feathered with my fate; he who in his hour
    Broke the irreparable dam which kept his thought,
    Released the cataract of birth and death
    To storm across time and the world;
    He who in his morning
    Drew open the furious petals of the sun;
    He who through his iron fingers
    Lets all go, lets all waste and go,
    Except, dearly retained in his palm, the soul:

He, the God of my living, the God of the Hebrews,
Has stooped beside Israel
And wept my life like a tear of passion
On to the iniquity of Egypt.

ANATH. So the great general steps down to captaincy.
I wonder. Does this god use you
Or do you use this god? What is this divinity
Which with no more dexterity than a man
Rips up good things to make a different kind
Of good? For any god's sake, if you came here
To get justice, also give justice.
In this mood the lot goes headlong.

MOSES.   Headlong!
And our memories too. And our hands which once
Knew how to come together, must now for ever
Hide themselves in our dress. We are utterly separate.

RAMESES. Look at the sky! A sea of cloud, blind-black,
Is pouring on to the beaches of the sun!

TEUSRET. Oh, it will swamp the sailing of the air!
The sky will be gone from us, it's taking the sky!
What shall we do?

ANATH.   Hush, Teusret.

                                        [*The stage grows dark*

MOSES.   Seti
May see better without the light of day.
The hand of God has gone across his eyes
And closed all life upon itself. Egypt
Goes inward, by a gate which shuts more heavily than sunset,

[73]

Leaving man alone with his baffled brain.
Only Seti can let the sun free again.

ANATH. It is here! The darkness!

MOSES.   Tell him, tell Seti
That I wait for his answer.

CURTAIN TO ACT TWO

ACT THREE

SCENE ONE

MIRIAM'S *tent at night.* AARON. *Enter* MIRIAM.

AARON. Everything has been done, I think. I have daubed
The lamb's blood three times over the entry
And all that remained of the meat has been burned.—
Miriam! You; not Moses! What do you want
Here at close on midnight?

MIRIAM.   Must I want something
To come into my own tent?

AARON.   Tell me; what is it?
There's no time left. Has the news got past our silence?
Do they know? That's why you've come in the night. The
    Egyptians
Are one ahead of us!

MIRIAM.   News? I've got no news.
Is there any news at midnight? I've come to sleep.

AARON. Why not sleep, as you did, in the city with Shendi?

MIRIAM. Do I have to be catechized in my own tent?
If you want to ferret in unlighted places
Penetrate into the mind of Moses, and let me
Sleep.

AARON. His mind will be our history
Before the morning. Whatever is about to happen—
I cannot doubt that something is about to happen—
Will divulge him to us at last. I have become

[75]

Almost docile to his darkness. By what providence
I wonder, did you come back? There was no way
Of getting word to you, but you came, thank God.
Whatever is wrong for you, to make you walk
So far to sleep, this midnight of Moses
(I call it to myself his midnight) will clarify
Into right.

MIRIAM.   Wrong things and right things!
So you still talk of those, those things that are catches
To make us lose heart. Take evil by the tail
And you find you are holding good head-downwards.
Let me go to sleep.

AARON.   Something that Shendi has done
Has brought you back.

MIRIAM.   Shendi, Shendi to blame!
To you Shendi is always blameable.
Because at last he can have ambitions,
Because he's ripping up the bare boards
His boyhood lay on, to make himself a fire
Which will warm his manhood, we turn on him—yes,
I also, as much as you—I stormed so.
I? The right to blame him? The wrong to have borne him
To that childhood. Why shouldn't he be finished with the lot of
    us?

AARON. So he turned you out: he sent you away.

MIRIAM.   I left him.
I came away from him. I couldn't watch him
Live what is now his life.

AARON.   I won't think of him.

MIRIAM. He'll succeed without your thoughts.

AARON.   Look at me, Miriam.

[76]

MIRIAM. You're going away.

AARON.   And so is all Israel.
We all have staves in our hands and our feet shod
For travelling; Moses' orders. He also gave
Other orders; they were very curious.
We have all had to eat lambs' flesh, seasoned
With bitter herbs. As I see it, Miriam,
That is his characteristic way of achieving
Unity among us, before the event,
That we should all fill this waiting time by doing
The same thing, however trivial. And then
We have splashed the blood three times over the doorways.
That is quite inexplicable. It is drying in the night air,
At this moment, while I speak. What happens, I ask myself,
When it is dry? It means our freedom. He has told me so.
Tonight we're to go free. And when I look at him
I have to permit myself a wonderful hope.

MIRIAM. He came back from Midian a madman.

AARON. His madness seems to be a kind of extended sanity.
But he tells me nothing, nothing is discussed or planned
Even with me, his lieutenant. And this closeness
Has hurt me, I won't try to deny it. And yet
He has me by the scruff of the heart and I ask
No questions. I've begun to believe that the reasonable
Is an invention of man, altogether in opposition
To the facts of creation, though I wish it hadn't
Occurred to me. I've been with Moses, watching
How in tent after tent he manipulated
Man upon man into consciousness. Though perhaps
They don't know of what they're conscious, any more than I do.
Except of the night; of the night, Miriam! I would swear
The night is dedicated to our cause.

[77]

You must have seen it: there's such a brightness,
Such a swingeing stillness, the sky has transfixed itself;
As though it hung with every vigorous star
On some action to be done before daybreak.

Enter SHENDI

SHENDI. Why must he be here?
I have something to say to you, mother.

MIRIAM.   Not any more
Tonight; nothing more said tonight. Go back
To your bed.

SHENDI.   Yes, you must listen!

AARON.   Listen to your tongue
Or your brotherly whip?

MIRIAM.   He knows already what we feel.
Now let him alone.

SHENDI.   Let him think what he likes. I have come
To you, not to him. We've taken so long to get
What at last we have: why must you spoil it? I know;
It was the spate of our tempers, gone again now.
If you go away from me, more than half the triumph
Is lost. You haven't been my mother for nothing.
I mean to see you happy.

MIRIAM.   I shall stay alone.

SHENDI. Oh, it's fantastic. What did you expect
My work to be? And how can we be scrupulous
In a life which, from birth onwards, is so determined
To wring us dry of any serenity at all?

MIRIAM. You must do as you must.

AARON.   But in the morning
He may wish he had chosen otherwise.

[78]

SHENDI.   What do you mean?
   Let me hear what you mean by that. Have you
   And your brother done some dirtiness against me
   To put me wrong with the Pharaoh? I know you'd founder me
   If you had the chance——

Enter MOSES

MOSES.   Get ready, Miriam. And you,
   Shendi. Get together all that you value.
   You won't come to this tent again.

MIRIAM.   Get ready?
   All that I value? What would that be, I wonder?
   Tell your delirium to be precise.

AARON. This midnight is his. For pity's sake believe it,
   Miriam. Then all our wills resolved into
   One Will——

SHENDI.   His, of course! The stupendous mischief
   Of the man! I beg your pardon if he no longer
   Rates himself as a man after living through
   The pestilences as though he owned them.
   You can blame him, not me, for the punishment
   I give the labourers. He makes them undisciplined
   With his raving of freedom which they'll never get.
   It's he, not I, who knits the darker and darker
   Frowns for Pharaoh—it's he who's the one for you
   To abominate, if anybody.

MOSES.   Be ready for journey.
   The time is prepared for us. What we were is sinking
   Under the disposition of what will be.
   Let it so dispose; let us not fondle our wrongs
   Because they're familiar. Now, as the night turns,

[79]

A different life, pitched above our experience
Or imagining, is moving about its business.
Tonight—Aaron, Miriam, Shendi—our slavery
Will be gone.

AARON.   Do you hear what he says?

MIRIAM.   What is he hiding?
There's something he knows.

AARON.   Something known by the night;
That was how it felt to me.

MIRIAM.   What is it you know?

MOSES.   The sound
Of God. It comes; after all, it comes. It made
The crucial interchange of earth with everlasting;
Found and parted the stone lips of this
Egyptian twilight in the speech of souls,
Moulding the air of all the world, and desiring
Into that shell of shadow, a man's mind—
Into my own.

AARON.   What was told? What was said?

SHENDI.   Oh, leave them
To excite each other. I'm going if you're not.

MOSES. Stay where you are. Do you deny voice
To that power, the whirler of suns and moons, when even
Dust can speak, as it does in Moses now?
It comes.
And by the welding of what loved me and what harmed me,
I have been brought to that stature which has heard.
Tonight, at midnight,
God will unfasten the hawk of death from his
Grave wrist, to let it rake our world,

Descend and obliterate the firstborn of Egypt,
All the firstborn, cattle, flocks, and men:
Mortality lunging in the midnight fields
And briding in the beds: a sombre visit
Such as no nation has known before. Upon
All Egypt! Only we who have the darkness
Here in our blood, under the symbol of blood
Over our doors, only we of Israel
Standing ready for the morning will be unvisited.

AARON. So this is what you know.

SHENDI.   What he wants, what he fondly
Imagines. Why did I follow you here
To get drawn into this? That fox has his tail on fire
And someone should know about it. For the last time,
Are you coming?

MIRIAM.   Don't go back—not just
Within a pace of this midnight.

SHENDI.   I can see
What's been thought out between you. Now that you have me,
You think you'll keep me: here, dropped back in the pit.
What chance of it! Must I tell you that I'm an Egyptian?
An Egyptian! I'm an Egyptian!

AARON.   Mind what you say, Shendi!
Remember the midnight promised to us,
Which is almost here! No doubt the timing of God
Will be extremely exact. And does nothing, no presentiment,
Creep on the heart of Pharaoh at this moment?

MOSES. Aaron!

AARON. I wonder, does nothing make him fetch his firstborn
Beside him——

[81]

MOSES.   Aaron!
   Do you see the ambush I have blundered into?
   I heard God, as though hearing were understanding.
   But he kept his hands hidden from me. He spoke,
   But while he spoke he pointed. Aaron, he pointed
   At Rameses, and I couldn't see!

AARON.   The boy
   Pays for the father.

MOSES.   Why had I not thought of him?—
   When other boys were slaughtered I was spared for Israel.
   Surely I who have been the go-between for God
   Can keep one firstborn living now for Egypt?

AARON. Is this how you fought your other wars?
   There were boys then who put
   Eager toes into fatal stirrups, who were young
   And out of life altogether in the same
   Almighty and unthinkable moment. You learnt
   Then to grieve and advance, uninterrupted.
   And so it has to be now.

MOSES.   Look what it is,
   God is putting me back with the assassins.
   Is that how he sees me? I killed an Egyptian
   And buried him in the sand. Does one deed then
   Become our immortal shape? And Egypt! Egypt!
   He was meant for Egypt. Aaron,
   You are here in my place until I come again.
   Keep Shendi with you.

AARON.   Where are you going?

MOSES. Keep Shendi with you.   [He goes

[82]

AARON. He is in a space somewhere between
   The human and inhuman. That's a terrible
   Neighbourhood.

SHENDI.   Did you see how he looked? He believes
   What he said.

MIRIAM.   Shut us in. He has gone.
   Can't we forget the man?

SHENDI.   I won't stay here!
   Thank goodness I can go where things are healthier.

AARON. It's midnight.
   Wasn't that the winding of the city's horn,
   The sound of twelve? I think so. I have to delay you,
   Shendi.

SHENDI [*at the tent-opening*]. Nobody will delay me.

MIRIAM.   Stay in the tent!

AARON. The hour may go past and leave us knowing
   It was unremarkable. But wait till the light,
   Wait, Shendi, keep yourself unseen
   By that inquisition of stars out there.
   Wait for Moses to return.

SHENDI.   Who?

MIRIAM. What is it? What have you seen?

SHENDI.   I've lost the city,
   I can't reach it! You trapped me!

MIRIAM.   What do you see?

SHENDI. The sand is rising and living!
   Is an invisible nation going through to the north
   Or what is it the sand can feel? I can't go back,
   God, God, I can't go!

[83]

MIRIAM.   Come inside,
  Shendi, come into the tent.

AARON.   Happening,
  You see, happening. Why try to go back?

SHENDI. Some of the men will still be awake. We could light
  The lights in the barrack-room. If only some of them
  Would come out to look for me! Can you hear it, the noise,
  The rending apart and shuddering-to of wings?
  Where can I get away from this? Nowhere
  Except into the ground.

MIRIAM.   Shendi, here, in the tent.
  In the tent: it will pass the tent.

AARON [*dragging him in*].   Are you trying to die?

SHENDI. Let me go, death; death, let me go!

AARON.   It is I
  Not death.

SHENDI.   It isn't only you.
  The wings were right over me and I was wrenched by a hand
  That came spinning out of them. I'll not be sent into a grave.
  I'll be what I was. I am Shendi, a Jew.
  How can my blood alter and make me Egyptian?
  I only wanted to be free!   [*He tears off the Egyptian uniform*
  Look: Egypt comes away—it's no part of me,
  It's easily off. This body is all I am—
  It is Shendi, the Jew, Shendi, Shendi, a Jew,
  A Jew! Isn't it so? Then why am I dying?

MIRIAM. You are not, Shendi; it's gone past us. There's nothing
    more.

AARON. Look, you're with us.

[84]

SHENDI. Only free to die?
This wasn't a world. It was death from the beginning.
Here's my name, without a man to it. My name!
Let me go. It's a chance! I'll make them see me. Wings,

[*He breaks away into the dark*

Shadows, eagles! I am Shendi, Shendi, the Jew!
I am Shendi the Jew! Shendi the Jew!

MIRIAM. Shendi!
He has gone behind the sand. Son! [*She runs into the dark*

AARON. The night
Of deliverance. Tonight we all go free.
And Miriam too. He said she would go free.

[*The voice of* MIRIAM *is heard crying out her last desperate*
'*Shendi!*'

CURTAIN

SCENE TWO

The Palace. ANATH. TEUSRET

ANATH. How the stars have taken possession of the sky tonight.

TEUSRET. Occasion, dear Aunt. Phipa is coming,
The magnitude out of Syria.

ANATH. Tomorrow.

TEUSRET. No; now they say tonight, very soon,
For Rameses. Messengers were here
Half an hour ago, sweating in the cool yard.
She's already at Hahiroth, with her romantic nature
Plying the spurs, and waking all the villages

[85]

With the interminable jingle-jangle of what father calls
Her considerable means. We shall see her tonight.

ANATH. How do we welcome her? Nothing has been said
To me.

TEUSRET. Who says anything in this palace now
Except good morning or good night? Father
Waits for each moment to come and touch him
And then it has gone before he can use it.

ANATH.   And you
Have a hard welcome for this girl from Syria.

TEUSRET. No; I'm praying her here, for all our sakes.
She will bring solid and gay Syria
To chase away the fiends.

Enter SETI

Who is that?

SETI. I. Is there something to be seen?

ANATH. We're watching the dark for bridles.

TEUSRET.   And the dark
Watches us. I know you dislike me to be afraid of it.
Are we all to meet her in the jumping shadows,
Aunts, owls, flame, sisters and all?
Or will she go quietly to bed and wait for tomorrow?

SETI. Tonight. She must dismount into a light
Of welcome. Where's your brother? . . . Turn this way;
Are you handsome? Well, the years of my life
Conveyed in a woman, perhaps safely. Remember to love me
For everything you become, particularly
For the worship of the male sunrise which will stand
Over your maturity.

[86]

TEUSRET. What is it, father?
  What is it?

SETI. How many thousand thousand years
  Are being nursed in your body, my young daughter?
  And under a secure lock, away from the eyes.

TEUSRET. What eyes?

SETI. The envy; confusion.
  Where's Rameses?

TEUSRET. In bed.

SETI. He can go to bed tomorrow.

ANATH. Precious heart,
  That was a wild cry that ripped the darkness
  From somewhere down in the city.

SETI. He will have dreams in plenty after tonight;
  I'm giving them to him with both my hands. Where is he?
  Fetch him.

RAMESES [in the doorway]. I am here, sir.

SETI. You're the Pharaoh.

ANATH. Seti!

SETI. You have slept into a throne and an empire
  While time has begun to heap age over me
  With a bony spade, to make me like the rest,
  Rameses, like the poor rest.

RAMESES. Has Syria come?

ANATH. Tell the boy what you mean: and me.
  What are you pulling down now?

SETI. Myself.
  It seems that I have grown too tall
  And keep out the sun. I overbranch the light.

[87]

I am giving you the throne, Rameses.
It gives itself. The wind has hurled it under you,
A biting wind, the hatred that has turned me
Into decay and grub in my own garden.
You may have luckier hands. You have at least
Hands less calloused with enemies. You will be able
To hold the sceptre perhaps without such pain.

ANATH. Abdication!

RAMESES.   Is that what you mean? The throne?

SETI. This is how we distract them: under my seal
    Affixed in the morning, Moses shall have the permission
    He has raged for: and then, with the sun somewhat higher,
    Under my final seal you shall take Egypt.
    I drown myself in my own wave: I am not,
    But I am always. And when they come, the factions,
    The whorers and devourers, roaring over
    The rocks of the dynasty, they'll only find
    Perpetual Egypt.

RAMESES.   I'm to inherit the kingdom
    Of desperate measures, to be not a self
    But a glove disguising your hand. Is there nowhere
    Where I can come upon my own shape
    Between these overbearing ends of Egypt?
    Where am I to look for life?

SETI.   What else
    Am I shaking over you but a wealth of life?
    Do you comprehend, this land, the bright wrists
    Of the world on which the centuries are bracelets,
    Is yours? And the heart of beauty out of Syria.
    Teusret, watch: is there anything to be seen?
    Any sound yet?—Stupidity, what would you have?

Love is the dominant of life, to which all our changes
Of key are subdued in the end. You will be able
To wander the winding and coitous passages
Of the heart, and be more than you could have prophesied
For yourself.

TEUSRET. Listen, listen!

SETI. Is it the girl?

TEUSRET. No, listen!

ANATH. A tortured gale, a gale
Of crying moving through the streets.

TEUSRET. Listen!
It's the noise of breaking lives.

SETI. What is it now?

RAMESES. What is it, Darkness? Why are you coming now?
For whom this time?

ANATH. Oh, make the city silent!

TEUSRET. Someone's coming: a shadow, a man,
Leaping for the terrace.

RAMESES. Let it come to me.
If I'm to have Egypt I'll have its treachery, too.
Keep away from the window. Who goes there? Stand.
Who goes there? Who is it?

[MOSES *comes breathlessly on to the terrace*

MOSES. Shut all your doors! Nothing will wait for us,
We are at war with this moment. Draw yourselves
Like swords. It is for Rameses.

RAMESES. For me?

MOSES. Put your lives round him.

SETI. Have you come
Out of the city? What's there? What's on its way?

MOSES. Death, death, deliberately
Aimed, falling on all your firstborn sons,
All Egypt's firstborn, Seti, cattle and men;
Death mounting with a growing storm of cries
To your window, to come to Rameses. I know—
It was I that loosed it. Can I deflect it now?
Can we so rope our lives together that we
Can be a miracle against death?

SETI. Go back
Into your night. I'll not believe in you.

ANATH. What do you want from us?

MOSES. Power of life
To beat death out of this house.
The vigour of our lives must be
The miracle to save him.

ANATH. What is my life?
It went to be your shadow. For fifteen years
It has been nothing but a level of darkness
Cast on the world by you. I made myself
Your mother, and then loved you and desired you
Till you became the best and worst of the world,
The water that kept me alive to thirst.

MOSES. Anath——

ANATH. I loved you until I longed to hear
That you were dead.

MOSES. Not this, not now!
Give me greater life for the boy's sake.

[90]

SETI. There is no more life to be demanded of me
Than I've already given: care,
Effort, devotion, sacrifice of all inclination,
Even to the sacrifice of my own person.
I have changed the channel that evil was running in.
This boy's the Pharaoh now.

RAMESES.   And yet,
If I'm to live, shall I know how?

MOSES. We'll hold you with our lives, if our lives will hold.
More life! The dark is already beside us.
In life's name, what are we?
Five worlds of separation? Or can we be
Five fingers to close into a hand
To strike this death clean away from us?
Has none of us the life to keep him living?

SETI. A great power, a great people,
A living Egypt.

MOSES.   Pain of man,
Affirm my strength, and make me
Equal to this wrestler come against me.

TEUSRET. Look, look—the torches in the gateway;
She is here!

SETI.   Anath, all of you,
We meet her as though Egypt were in high health;
No anxiety on your faces as though you were ambassadors
Of some haunted country.

TEUSRET.   We shall be alive again.
Phipa has come to us, and the horns have begun
To wind their welcome in the towers. Come on,

[91]

Rameses, come to meet her. The dark's not dangerous
Now.

RAMESES. But still dark. And we have to enact
A daylight for this unsuspecting beauty.
Well, we'll meet her.

ANATH.   No, don't go, don't look!
The men who were opening the gates to let her in
Have fallen to the ground. An owl in mid-air
Has wrenched itself upward screaming, and smashed
Down to the yard—there falls another! Oh,
Are these the flowers we throw at her feet?
You asked us for life, Moses; what life have you
Against this death which pushes through the gate
Shoulder to shoulder with the bride? Moses,
It is now that you must break through to your power,
Now! It's here.

MOSES.   The shadows are too many.
All was right, except this, all, the reason,
The purpose, the justice, except this culmination.
Good has turned against itself and become
Its own enemy. Have we to say that truth
Is only punishment? What must we say
To be free of the bewildering mesh of God?
Where is my hand to go to? Rameses,
There's no more of me than this. This is all:
I followed a light into a blindness.

TEUSRET.   Come
Away, Rameses, Rameses, come now.
You must meet her and love her.
Isn't it in love that life is strongest?
I want you to love her. Already we're late.

[92]

RAMESES. Why is she sighing, Teusret? Such great sighs.
They have taken all the air. Now there will be
Nowhere to breathe. Come with me.

> [*He crumples and falls*

TEUSRET.   Rameses,
I don't know the way!

RAMESES.   I am finding it for you.
Stoop, Teusret. You see? You cannot lose me.
Here I am. [*He dies.*]

TEUSRET.   Where? Where? Rameses!
I'll meet her alone, then. When she comes she'll reach you.
She must, she must. She came so far.

> [*She runs to the courtyard*

ANATH. Rameses, pharaoh of sleep, you have
The one sure possession of the world.

SETI [*to* MOSES]. You have done what you returned for.
You found us in the morning.
Leave us with what remains of the night.
The day you found us in is over.

Enter AARON

AARON. We are standing ready. The sound of the wings is quiet
And the stars are fading in silence.
All ears wait for your command to march.
Egypt is throwing away its gold to have us gone.
Is it now?

MOSES.   Now! At last the crying of our past
Is over.

ANATH. You have the freedom of the darkness, Moses.
Why do you wait? Haven't you recognized
The triumph of your purpose? Your twelve hundred

[93]

Thousand souls, out there in the dungeon of the night,
Are waiting to hear the long bolts grate back.
Rameses has died,
And the air stands ready in the wilderness to take you in.
Rameses has died. Tomorrow the lizards
Will be sparkling on the rocks. Why aren't you dancing
With such liberty for such starving souls?

MOSES. Anath—Egypt,
Why was it I that had to be disaster to you?
I do not know why the necessity of God
Should feed on grief; but it seems so. And to know it
Is not to grieve less, but to see grief grow big
With what has died, and in some spirit differently
Bear it back to life. The blame could impale me
For ever; I could be so sick of heart
That who asked for my life should have it; or I could see
Man's life go forward only by guilt and guilt.
Then we should always be watching Rameses die.
Whereas he had such life his death can only
Take him for a moment, to undo his mortality,
And he is here pursuing the ends of the world.

ANATH. You have nothing now except the wilderness.

MOSES. The wilderness has wisdom.
And what does eternity bear witness to
If not at last to hope?

Re-enter TEUSRET

TEUSRET.   I have seen her. O Rameses,
She has come so gifted for you,
With pearls like seeds of the moon,
With metal and strange horns, ebon and ivory,
Spilling chalcedonyx and male sapphires.

[94]

Doesn't their brightness come to you? Do they glimmer
Nowhere into the cupboards of your sleep?

SETI. She need bring nothing, except the hour that has gone.

MOSES. Death and life are moving to a call.
I turn from Egypt.

ANATH. What is left
To call to me?

MOSES. The morning, which still comes
To Egypt as to Israel, the round of light
Which will not wheel in vain.
We must each find our separate meaning
In the persuasion of our days
Until we meet in the meaning of the world.
Until that time.

[*He goes. The early light reaches* RAMESES

THE CURTAIN FALLS

THE PLAY ENDS

THOR, WITH ANGELS

First performed at the Canterbury Festival in June 1948.
First published in an acting edition by H. J. Goulden Ltd.
for the Friends of Canterbury Cathedral in 1948.
Reissued by the Oxford University Press in 1949

CHARACTERS

CYMEN

CLODESUIDA, *His Wife*

MARTINA, *His Daughter*

QUICHELM, *His Elder Son*

CHELDRIC, *His Younger Son*

TADFRID ⎱
OSMER ⎰ *His Brothers-in-Law*

COLGRIN, *His Steward*

ANNA, *Colgrin's Wife*

HOEL, *A British Prisoner*

MERLIN

A MESSENGER

SCENE: *A Jutish Farmstead*, A.D. 596

A Jutish farmstead, both within and without. To the left a group of trees; to the right a shed, in which COLGRIN, *an elderly man, is asleep among the straw. Enter* QUICHELM. *He hammers at the farm door.*

QUICHELM. Hyo, there! Who's awake? Where's
The welcome of women for warfarers?
Where's my Wodenfearing mother?
Hey! hey! Spare some sleep for us:
Leave us half a snore and a stale dream.
Here's your battery of males come home!
Our bones are aching; we're as wet
As bogworms. Who's alive in there?

COLGRIN. There's an infernal clatter. What's the matter?
Foof! Straw in the nostrils. That's bad.
Who's blaspheming in the thick of the mist?
I've got you on my weapon's point.
(Where the Valhalla is it?)

QUICHELM.   Colgrin,
You scrawny old scurfscratcher, is that you?

COLGRIN. Frog-man, fen-fiend, werewolf, oul, elf,
Or whatever unnatural thing you are
Croaking in the voice of Master Quichelm
Who I happen to know is away waging war,
Stand away from the swiping of my sword.
(Where in thunder did I put it?)

QUICHELM. Runt of an old sow's litter, you slop-headed
Pot-scourer, come here, you buckle-backed
Gutsack, come out of there!

COLGRIN.   That's
The young master. There's not a devil
In the length of the land could pick such a posy of words

And not swoon smelling it. Here I come,
Here I come. Welcome home and so forth.

QUICHELM. Woden welt you for a sheeptick, where's my mother?

COLGRIN. That's a nice question. I must ponder.
Maybe asleep in her cot. Or not.

QUICHELM. I'll carve your dropsical trunk into a tassel.
Where's my sister? You were left to guard them,
Not to roll your pig-sweat in a snoring stupor.
Tell me where they are before I unbutton your throat.

MARTINA [*entering*]. We're here, Quichelm. I knew you'd come
to-day.
The cows this morning were all facing north.
Are you whole and hale?

QUICHELM.   Look me over. Ten
Fingers. You can take the toes for granted.
Where's my mother?

MARTINA.   We went to early rite.
I wanted to stay and keep a watch out for you
But she made me go; you know what she is.

COLGRIN. That's what I said. Gone to early rite.
And my wife with her; a devout woman, but dismal
In some respects. They'll be back just now.
The sun's arisen.

QUICHELM.   You get stuck
Into some work, you whitebellied weasel.
By dugs, I think I'll strike you anyway.

COLGRIN. Wasn't I there as bright and bristling
As Barney the boarhound, just as soon as I heard
Your honour's foot creak over the bridge?

[102]

MARTINA. Beat him to-morrow. Let's be affable.
Is father all right? And Cheldric?

QUICHELM.   Cheldric's all right.

MARTINA. Why not father? Stop picking at your teeth.
Something is wrong. Was father killed?
I knew it. The house was crowned with crows this morning.

QUICHELM. Shut up. None of us is killed.
Are you still here?

COLGRIN [*going in*]. No, sir, no. It's what
You remember of me. There's trouble coming. I see that.

Enter CLODESUIDA *and* ANNA.

CLODESUIDA. Quichelm, you're back! Oh, fortunate day.

ANNA. Welcome home.

QUICHELM.   Yes, the battle's finished.

CLODESUIDA [*to* ANNA]. Rouse the fire up; and find them food.
                                              [*Exit* ANNA.

MARTINA. Don't expect pleasure.

CLODESUIDA.   Something is wrong. Is your father
With you, and well?

QUICHELM.   He's much as when you saw him.

CLODESUIDA. Much? What's that, much? Has he been hurt?

QUICHELM. No weapon has touched him.

CLODESUIDA.   Then he's ill?
Why do you talk to me in a kind of cloud?
What has happened?

QUICHELM.   Mother, we breathe cloud.
It's the chief product of this island.

[103]

CLODESUIDA.   Don't provoke me!
   Where is your father?

QUICHELM.   Coming up the hill.

MARTINA. Dimly, yes; I can just see the shapes of them.

CLODESUIDA. And Cheldric, too? And your uncles?
   Yes,
   They all come. The mist is confusing. I could imagine
   There are five of them.

QUICHELM.   So there are. My father
   Brings a prisoner.

CLODESUIDA.   A prisoner? Are we
   To have an intolerable Saxon here?

QUICHELM. An even greater strain on your toleration:
   A Briton. A British slave who fought for the Saxons.

CLODESUIDA. But why? Why bring a benighted Briton here?
   I thought those heathen had been tidied away, once
   And for all. And the country's healthier for it.
   Your father's demented.

QUICHELM.   You would have said so
   If you had seen him as we saw him in the battle.
   Like a madman, he saved this Briton when we'd have killed him:
   Burst in among us, blaspheming against Woden,
   Broke his sword in the air—he swore it broke
   Against a staggering light—and stood roaring,
   Swaying in a sweat of wax, bestraddled
   Over the fallen Briton. And then, as though
   The beast which had bragged in his brain had leapt away,
   Became himself again,
   Only in a fury with the light which broke his sword.

CLODESUIDA. How could the sword have broken?

[104]

You make me afraid
To see him. Are you sure that he blasphemed?
That's the worst of all. It's hard enough
To live well-thought-of by the gods.

MARTINA.   We haven't
Enough cattle to placate them more than twice a year.
He knows we have to be careful.

QUICHELM. They're here. And you haven't heard the worst.

CLODESUIDA. The worst? What worse can there be?
      Quichelm,
What else? . . .

QUICHELM. Don't let him know that I've been talking.
He'd lay me flat.

CLODESUIDA. He'll notice how I tremble.

      [*Enter to the house* CYMEN, *his brothers-in-law* TADFRID
      and OSMER, *and his younger son* CHELDRIC. CLODE-
      SUIDA *and* MARTINA *stand staring at him.*

CYMEN. Well? Have I come home? Or is this a place
Of graven images? What's the silence for?
I've laid down arms, so that arms
Could take me up, a natural expectation.
Where's my wife?

CLODESUIDA. You can see me. Here I am.

CYMEN. Where's my wife? Where's the head on my breast?
Better. Where's my daughter? Where's the white
Hand hanging on my shoulder? Better, better.
I'll have a cup of mead.
Where's my mead? Where the devil's my mead?
Have I got to wring the water out of my shirt
To get a drink?

COLGRIN [*appearing*]. Here's your mead, my lord:
And the bees were proud to make themselves drunk
To make you drunk, and welcome home, my lord,
And Woden worship you and your victory,
Hear, hear!

CYMEN.   Loki lacerate you for a liar
And my foot in your teeth.

COLGRIN.   Quite so, exactly.

CYMEN. Wash my feet. Well, here's gut-comfort, anyway.
Who can be called defeated who can still imbibe
And belch?

CLODESUIDA. Defeated? Have you come back defeated
When I sacrificed a good half-goat. . . .

CYMEN.   No doubt
The wrong half, my jewel: the hind-quarters,
And it brought us rumping home. Well,
I'm still good enough for a bad joke.
Liquor. Down the throat, sunshine; hum
A lazy day to my inside. I'll doze
In the meadow of my stomach. There's no warmth in a wife.

CLODESUIDA. Who turns me cold? What besides defeat
Have you still to tell me?

CYMEN.   Ask the dumb icebergs behind you.
Take stock of those long jowls, my jewel,
Those ruminating thundercoloured bulls
Your brothers: and our pastry-pallid sons
Who look on their father with such filial
Disapproval. A fine resentful march
This night has been, with no moon and no
Conversation: nothing to break the monotony
Except Tadfrid spitting once in every mile

And twenty-seven gurks from Osmer.
Spit some words at me instead, and gurk
Away your grudge. I'm tired of this subterranean
Muttering. Where's that water? My feet want comfort.

TADFRID. That's what this house will want before long, and may
Our guilt be forgiven us.

CLODESUIDA. What kind of talk is this?

CYMEN. Tell her, tell her. I'm humble.

CLODESUIDA. Do you say that?
Guilt, forgiveness, humility? What next?
Are you mad?

CYMEN. Tell her I am or you'll strangle yourselves
With an unspoken truth.

CLODESUIDA. Has none of you the courage
To speak?

TADFRID. Even though he's our overlord,
And though he may not at the time have been fully responsible—

OSMER. Let me tell her, Tadfrid; I speak faster.
It was approaching dusk, last evening.
We were catching a bright victory in our caps,
When Eccha, the earl, was killed by a thrust from the spear
Of this British brat:
And we were at the boy in the bat of an eye
To give him joy of our vengeance and a shove
To doom and a damned journey into dust,
When Cymen, our chief, our lord, your maleficent
Male—

CLODESUIDA. Though you're my brother I'll beat your mouth
If it passes a lie!

TADFRID. It's the truth that he says.

[107]

OSMER. All right.
It's the truth that I say. Like a bear-sark blundering
He hit up our downcoming swords, sprang in
As white as a water-spout spinning in a full moon,
Shouting 'The gods can go and beg for blood!
Let 'em learn of us!'

TADFRID. Word for word. 'Let 'em learn
Of us.'

CLODESUIDA. It's certain they heard!

OSMER. From that moment, you
could feel it,
The sky turned round, Ceaulin's men broke through,
Thor, in the scarlet dusk, swore and swung,
And Woden rode in rancour, as well he might,
And trod upon our dead.

TADFRID. And so we slogged
Out from defeat, and he lugged the Briton with him.

CLODESUIDA. Is it believable?

CHELDRIC. Look, father's weeping.

QUICHELM. A nice inheritance we have, all watermarked
With tears.

CLODESUIDA. Who's this man, spilling sawdust
Like an old puppet? I never saw him till now.
You make me ashamed, in front of our sons.

CYMEN. Can't I
Have tears of rage? Why not the hot spout
Of indignation? Is it better to spew?
By the thousand and three thews of the muscular god,
Some fiend of this land came at my back!
I was thrown by a trick.

[108]

TADFRID.   He should stand in the winter sea
    Till his clothes freeze to his flesh. It's the only way
    To be sure of a store of magic against such an evil.

CLODESUIDA. And catch death? That's an efficacious magic
    If you like. It's more decently religious
    To offer a sacrifice, than to offer himself
    To an early grave.

OSMER.   What devil was it that damned him
    To its own design? Can he tell us that?

CYMEN.   Some ancient
    Damp god of this dooming island, who spat
    The fungus out of his mouth and caught me napping.
    I curse this kingdom, water, rock and soil!
    I accuse and curse the creaking of its boughs
    And the slaver on the mouth of its winds! It makes
    A fool of me! Too many voices rasp
    Out of decaying rafters, out of every cave
    And every hole in the yellow sodden hills.
    This is the golden future our fathers died for!
    The gods look at it! Here's the slice of fortune
    They came to carve with their courage
    When they pitched themselves on the narrow, shuddering sea
    To deal and duck death under the hanging chalk.
    I stack my curses on those first rich rumours
    Which fetched us here, rollicking with ambition.
    I curse the muck and gravel where we walk.
    I'd curse each singular soaking blade of grass
    Except that a grey hair ties me for time.
    Here we live, in our fathers' mirage.
    Cities, they'd heard of, great with columns,
    Gay cities, where wealth was bulging the doors
    And the floors were sagging with the weight of gold.

The orchards rang with fruit, the hills moved
With grain like a lion's mane, and wherever
A river sauntered the fish swam, and eels
Reeled in bright mud. Flocks were fair,
And cows like pendulous fountains of alabaster
Went lowing over land where silver skulked
Waiting for skill; a land where summer days
Could call to one another across the night
Under the northern pole. So here we live
And choke in our father's mirage. Dreams they were,
As well we know; we live in the skull
Of the beautiful head which swam in the eyes of our fathers.
Our ploughshares jag on the stumps of moonwhite villas.
And my brain swerves with the sudden sting of one
Of the island gods, the down-and-out divinities
Moping, mildewed with immortality,
Cross-boned on weedy altars. I curse this land
That curses me!

OSMER.   Then cut yourself clear of its curse
And win this house again for Woden, before
We all know worse.
                    [*He drags forward* HOEL, *the Briton.*
                    Here's the land you loathe,
In bone and blood. Break its back.

CLODESUIDA.   We have always
Been god-fearing, but now it appears he fears
More gods than he knows what to do with. What can we do?

TADFRID. Obliterate the cause of sin. Do the undeed,
The death-lack which lost us our victory.
Where's the difficulty?

OSMER.   There is no difficulty.
Here's the quivering black-haired flesh,

[110]

As live as it was that time our blades were on him.
Well, we swing back on time, and hope the gods
Forget the indecision.

TADFRID.   It may seem now
To be somewhat in cold blood, but in fact his death
Was given to him in the battle yesterday;
This is merely the formal ceremony, which was overlooked.

QUICHELM. Kill him; make us respectable again.
I feel that all the gods are looking at us.

CHELDRIC. Do, father, kill him, as any other fellow's
Father would.

CLODESUIDA. Not inside the house!
The walls would never let his death go out.

CYMEN. No, nor anywhere here, I'll tell you all
Darker things yet. I have a great fear.

CLODESUIDA. Fear? Will you say that to the ears of your sons?

CYMEN. I say I fear myself, or rather
That not-myself which took my will,
Which forced a third strange eye into my head
So that I saw the world's dimensions altered.
I know no defence against that burst of fire.
[_To_ HOEL.] You can tell me; what flogged away my strength,
What furtive power in your possession
Pulled the passion of my sword? Name that devil!
I'll have our gods harry him through the gaps
Between the stars, to where not even fiends
Can feed. Name him!

HOEL.   Who? Who am I to name?
I swear to God I know nothing of what you mean.

CYMEN. What God is that? You swear to a God?
What God?

[111]

HOEL. It was my grandfather who knew him well.
The One God, he's called. But I can't remember
The details; it's a long time ago that I saw
My grandfather, and I'm the last life
Of my family.

OSMER.   Send him where the moles
Can teach him to dig in the dark.

TADFRID.   His brows are marked
With the night already; douse the rest of him
And let's get to bed.

CYMEN.   Why shouldn't we give you the mercy
You showed to Eccha our earl?

HOEL.   It was all in the way
Of battle. I only expelled him from the world
As I let out my breath singing to the fame
Of Britain.

TADFRID. The fame of Britain! The fame of Britain
Is sung by us now. Let him echo Eccha
Into death, with the same ease.

OSMER.   Easy death,
Easy as shutting a door!

CYMEN.   This door shan't shut
Till I find what devil keeps it.

OSMER.   Then, by plague,
I'll void my vows of allegiance to this damned house!

TADFRID. And I; like a rat I'll run
Before the water rises.

CLODESUIDA.   Do you forget
Your wife and children? A sacrifice, Cymen,
This one sacrifice for our peace of mind.

CYMEN. What peace can we have until I know
  Whether or not the same misshapen fire again
  Will burn me? I've still got rags of reason
  To make our stark apprehension decent,
  And you shall be modest with me, or else bad-luck
  Will leer at the lot of us. If we kill him and bury him,
  I shall fill my lungs with relief and forget my fault
  And the flame will be on me while I whistle at a clear sky.
  No! This walking wound in my strength can walk on,
  Wake me in the morning, see me to my bed;
  He shall stand between me and the door so that his shadow
  Falls across everything I do: so every
  Moment shall have spears addressed to that dark
  Which lies in wait for my will. Alive,
  He's ours; dead, who knows to what
  Unfriendly power he will have given himself?
  Scowl at your own stampede of panic,
  Not at me. Look; the sun puts down
  The mist at last and looks out across the day.
  Here comes the burning sea of honey
  Over the grey sand of our defeat.
  We'll salute the sun that makes us men.
  Fill up the cups! [*To* COLGRIN.]
  O gigantic heart, beating in the breast of the sky,
  Lordlust the white-hot lion of the air,
  We are the men of the earth; our metal shouts
  With light only for you. (For chick's sake,
  Fill 'em up, fill 'em up!)—
  Give us huge harvest, potency and dominion.
  Make us pluck all from the teeth of this island.
  My strength comes back. By splendour,
  I'll send fear sprawling. By the zenith, I'll set
  My foot on the neck of the dark and get the gods

Again. [*He throws* HOEL *to the ground and puts his foot on his neck.*]
         Glory of life, I live!
We'll drink to our restored prosperity:
The sustaining sinews of tremendous Thor:
The unwearying, turbulent, blazing loins of Woden!
We raise our cups and drink, to the power of the gods,
This toast:
                    'Let us love one another.'
                    [*His cup falls from his hand. He stands trembling.*

OSMER. What madness is this?

CLODESUIDA.   What words are these?

TADFRID.   He has fallen
    Foul of his brain again, protect us!

CHELDRIC.   'Let us
    What,' did father say?

QUICHELM.   'Love one another';
    What a way to honour the gods!

CLODESUIDA.   He's not himself.
    It's the patter of delirium he talks;
    A lack of sleep.

CYMEN.   I'm in good health!
    No-one shall excuse this fiend that twists my tongue,
    By saying I'm sick! Show, show, show,
    Devil! By the first yowl of the world's first babe
    I'll be the master of my own voice!
    Show! Come out of your secret place and let me
    See you climb to my sword. This time it means
    Death, your precious Briton's end, I kill him!
             [*He makes to kill* HOEL, *but his sword is against* QUIC-
             HELM.]

QUICHELM. Father!

CLODESUIDA.　　　　No! Hold him! He's battle-blind.

OSMER. You madman, it's your son, Quichelm. What's
The matter? Here's the road you have to take,
The black-haired enemy. Turn here.

CYMEN.　　　　　　　　　　　　It seems
All one, it seems all one. There's no distinction.
Which is my son?

QUICHELM.　　　　Can't you see me?
I'm your son.

CYMEN.　　　And my enemy,
My own flesh. My sword knew you. Deny it:
My sword understood. Distinction has gone!

CLODESUIDA. Take him and make him sleep; it must be
The burning of his body. I'll not believe
He is mad. Get him to rest and sleep. Dip him
In sleep, that blue well where shadows walk
In water over their heads, and he'll be washed
Into reason. This has taken my strength, too.

CYMEN. All right, I'll sleep. I'll count myself as over
For a while. But let not you, not one of you,
Step between me and what's to come. This house
Is on my back; it goes my way. Dare nothing
Against the Briton, or dread will stay with you
Forever, like pock-marks. We'll master this mystery,
His death can keep; his death can wait for me.
　　　[*Exeunt* CLODESUIDA, CYMEN, QUICHELM, CHELDRIC.

OSMER. And we're kept jangling in the pocket of uncertainty
While Woden wonders how to spend us.

TADFRID.　　　　　　　　　　　And sleep
Will lay us open to all the supernatural riffraff

[115]

That ever came crawling out of cobwebs. Pleasant
Dreams.

OSMER [*to* COLGRIN]. Take him to the barn.
Hanging for you, if he escapes.

COLGRIN. A rope isn't my style. I haven't the neck for it.
[*Exeunt* OSMER *and* TADFRID.

COLGRIN. Lowest form of life; that's you. Next to lowest, me.
So you can show respect. We'll make the barn
A guard-room. Get inside. This dizzy-dazzy
World made of morning sun and fog-spittle
Is nothing to do with you. Orders are otherwise.

HOEL. Try to think of it: I might by now
Have been wading about in the sway of death,
But I'm blinking at the light; my head swims with it.

COLGRIN. It doesn't do a man any good, daylight.
It means up and doing, and that means up to no good.
The best life is led horizontal
And absolutely unconscious. Get inside!
You flick of muck off the back hoof of a mule!
There's a point in being sworn at; it gives you something
To hand on to your fellow men. Now mind,
No monkey-tricks, no trying to escape,
I've got you covered—if I knew where I'd put my weapon.

HOEL. Where do you think I should escape to?

COLGRIN.   Why,
You'd skit off home.

HOEL.   That's where I've just escaped from
When I escaped death. Here I lie—
Hanging on to what was once my country,
Like an idiot clinging to the body of his dead mother.
Why don't you hack me off her? Why don't you?

[116]

Fool I was, fool I was, not to hug their swords
When they bore down on me. Why don't I settle
To a steady job in the grave, instead of this damned
Ambition for life, which doesn't even offer
A living wage? I want to live, even
If it's like a louse on the back of a sheep, skewering
Into the wool away from the beaks of crows;
Even like a limpet on a sour rock.
I want to live!

COLGRIN.   Me too;
Horizontal and absolutely unconscious.
But they keep us at it, they keep us at it.

                    Enter ANNA.

ANNA. Who at it? Not you at it. Don't you
Think he's ever at it; nobody's at it
Except old Anna. The farm's a hive
Of indolence: the place might as well be rubble.
Six upstanding men lying down, and nine
Cows lowing themselves into a cream cheese.
            [*She goes into the barn to take down the washing from where
            it hangs on* COLGRIN'S *sword stuck in a post.*
I won't say you're in my way
But I can't get to where I want to come to.

COLGRIN [*to* HOEL]. My only wife!

ANNA.   I'll take these into the sun.
Nothing ever dries in this country.

COLGRIN.   There's my weapon!
There's my dimpled sword! What do you mean, woman,
Hanging wet linen all over it? It's wrong
If it's rusty.

ANNA.   And a man is, too; and you're
So thick with rust you'd choke if you blew on yourself.

[117]

COLGRIN. I'm on special duty, Anna; I'm put to guard
A sad and savage Briton.

ANNA.   He needn't think
He'll be savage with me. He's caused a lot of trouble
Having to be conquered, and that's enough from him.
I shall probably get to be fond of him, but I'll never
Like him. It wouldn't be right if I did, when you think
Of all our men who've been killed killing these heathen.
And *this* isn't going to get the baby washed.

COLGRIN. What baby washed?

ANNA.   Can't I coin a phrase if I want to?
[*Exit* ANNA. *Enter* MARTINA *carrying an empty bowl.*

COLGRIN. My sword for a clothes-line!
Stand to attention. Here's my lord's daughter
Look as though you're working.

HOEL.   At what?

COLGRIN.   Here,
Plait some straw.

MARTINA.   Good morning, Colgrin.

COLGRIN.   Good-morning.
It's a bright day, lady, for the season.

MARTINA. Time, too. They made us wait for it.
I'm old with being young in a long winter.
I've almost forgotten how to walk on flowers.

COLGRIN. Everything would be all right if we'd been granted
Hibernation.

MARTINA.   We're not very favoured. The gods
Mean us to know they rule. Are your gods any
Kinder, Briton?

[118]

HOEL.   When I was a boy I was only
   Allowed to have one, though in that One, they said,
   There were three. But the altars are broken up. I've tried
   To pick away the moss to read the inscriptions
   But I've almost forgotten our language. I only know
   The god was both father and son and a brooding dove.

MARTINA. He's a Christian, Colgrin; and if you ask my mother
   She'll tell you that's worse than having no god at all.
   We have a Christian queen, though we try to keep it
   Dark, and in one of our prayers to the gods we say
   Give us our daily bread and forgive us our Queen.
   But we drove the Britons into the mountains; for years
   They've lain furtively in the setting sun,
   Those who live. Why aren't you lurking there, too?
   You should be crouching craven in a cave
   Warming your hands at the spark of your old god
   Who let you be conquered.

HOEL.   After my father was killed
   The Saxons kept me to work for them. My father
   Had always said What can one god do
   Against the many the invaders have?
   And he remembered earlier gods who still
   Harped on the hills, and hoped they would rally again.
   But they were too old. They only raised
   Infatuated echoes, and wept runnels.
   Then all the Britons were killed or fled, all
   Except my grandfather and my hip-high self.
   Him they kept for working metals which he did
   With his whole heart, forgetting the end of his race
   In a brooch design. He told me once
   How I'd been given in water to the One god.
   Soon afterwards he died, beating silver.

[119]

When I had grown the Saxons let me fight for them
And gave me a little freedom in exchange.

MARTINA. Enough for my father to take from you.
It's a pity
You had to be born a Briton. I'm forced to hate you.

HOEL. If I had been a Saxon . . .

MARTINA.   We should have killed you
To win your land, but considered you a brother.

COLGRIN. We should have killed you with consideration.
It isn't less fatal, of course, but it adds an air
Of glory, and we shake hands in Valhalla.

Enter CLODESUIDA.

CLODESUIDA. Martina, come, if you please! Two hands aren't
enough
To card and spin, and my brain goes with the wheel
Round and round in a horrible suspense.
What are you doing?

MARTINA.   Watching the herons. I'm coming.
They haunt the dregs of the mist like ghosts
Left on the yellow morning by a tide of sleep.

CLODESUIDA. Where did you take the bowl of meat?

MARTINA.   Where?

CLODESUIDA. I saw you come back from that old decaying
Tooth of a tower. And here's a string
Of bramble on your skirt, and burrs, and cleavers.
What were you doing there?

MARTINA.   I go very often.
Particularly when the house is overbearded
With splendid uncles.

CLODESUIDA.   Carrying a bowl of food?

[120]

MARTINA. Mother, I have to eat.

CLODESUIDA.   Do you have to eat
Among bird-droppings and birds' bones and beaks
And owl-chawn mice and dead flies? Is that
Nicer than your uncles? The tower's a spitting-place
For all benighted life, a filthy ruin.
You have someone hidden there.

MARTINA.   Suppose I have . . .

CLODESUIDA. I do suppose you have; and I shall find who.
I wear myself out securing us to the gods
With every device that's orthodox, sacrificing
To the hour, to the split minute of the risen sun.
But how can I keep them kind if always
They're being displeased by the rest of you? It isn't
Easy to keep on the windy side of Woden
As anyone knows. Who have you hidden in the ruin?

MARTINA. Hardly anyone at all. A very old man:
Old enough to be his own grandfather.

CLODESUIDA. But why—

MARTINA.   I dug him up. He was rather buried.
I found him in the quarry where it caved in.
His beard was twisted like mist in the roots of an oak-tree,
Beaded and bright with a slight rain, and he was crying
Like an old wet leaf. His hands were as brown as a nest
Of lizards, and his eyes were two pale stones
Dropping in a dark well. I thought I couldn't
Very well leave him where he was.

CLODESUIDA.   You should
Have left him, until we could find out more about him.
Is he natural? Is he good or evil? Out of the quarry!
He might be as fatal as a toadstool.

[121]

MARTINA. Maybe, maybe,
Maybe. He comforts me.

CLODESUIDA. He comforts you!
In what way, comfortable? Now we come to it.
What does he do?

MARTINA. He screws up his eyes and looks
At my hand and tells my future. It's better
Than always having to placate the gods
For fear something should happen. Besides, I like
To know. He says, as far as he can remember,
Though he has a terrible memory for names,
His name is Merlin.

HOEL [to COLGRIN]. What did she say?

COLGRIN. She said
I was so thick with rust I'd choke if I blew.
My sword for a clothes-line!

HOEL. Merlin!

CLODESUIDA. I only hope
He has done no harm to us yet, whatever he is,
Whatever his tongue clinks at, sitting with the rats.
It's no good having gods at the door if there
Are devils on the hearth. Your uncles, one or both,
Shall see him.

HOEL. She calls him Merlin. She has caught
An echo that booms in the deepest cave of my race
And brings it here, out into the winter light!

MARTINA. You shall see him for yourself.
Here he comes, with the red earth still on him
And his beard springing surprises on the breeze.
He promised not to break his hiding. Well,
You see how old he is. And how confused in the sun.
With two days' growth of shadow from the tower.

[122]

Enter MERLIN.

You've broken faith. You promised you'd lie low.

                    [MERLIN *moves on towards* HOEL.

CLODESUIDA. What is he after?

MERLIN [*to* HOEL].   Ail i'r ar ael Eryri
  Cyfartal hoewal a hi. Ar oror wir arwa.

HOEL. Peth yw . . . peth yw . . . I can't remember
  How to speak. I use the words of the Saxons.

CLODESUIDA. Another heathen! Did you know he was a Briton?
  Is that why you hid him from me?

MERLIN [*to* HOEL].   A British voice.
  It breaks a fast of years; I roll you
  Wonderfully on my tongue. I was half asleep
  But I heard you. This wide harp of winter
  Reverberates. I had stupidly imagined
  The human landscape had left me for ever.
  The face of the foam for me (I told myself)
  Until I die. All your expectation
  Of friendship, old man (I said to myself)
  Is a wink from the eye of a bullfinch
  Or the slower solemnities of a tortoise
  Or a grudging goodnight from the dark lungs of a toad.
  And then your voice alights on my ear. I bless you
  From the bottom of my slowly budding grave.

CLODESUIDA. You must speak to my brothers before we let you
    wander
  All over our land.

HOEL.   Madam, this may be Merlin.
  Still Merlin. Do you understand?

MERLIN. You are surprised, I see, to find me still
  Giving and taking the air. You think I should long ago

[123]

Have sunk to the golden bed of the troubled river.
But I have obstreperous garments that keep me floating.
I merely float, in a desultory, though
Delighted, kind of way. And my garments begin
To be heavy. Presently, on the surface of life,
You may observe a doting bubble, smiling
Inanely at the sun until it dissolves,
And then you'll know the time has been.

HOEL. It has gone
Already for us. We're lost and scattered.

MERLIN. Be lost
And then be found. It's an old custom of the earth
From year to year. I could do something;
But I lost my trumpet of zeal when Arthur died
And now I only wind a grey note
Of memory, and the hills are quiet.

CLODESUIDA. Did you hear
What I said to you?

MARTINA. Father has come from the house.

Enter CYMEN.

CLODESUIDA. Oh, you should be sleeping.

CYMEN. No sleep came.
An occasional shadow across my bed from a cloud
Of weariness, but the glare of the brain persisted.
Where is the Briton?

CLODESUIDA. There in the barn, there,
Talking to an old man of his tribe, or an old
Sorcerer, or some brewer of trouble.
We should rid the country of these things which aren't ourselves.

[124]

CYMEN. Rid the brain of uncertainty, rid the heart
Of its fear.

[*He goes to the barn.*

How did this old man come here?
The kingdom has been scoured of you islanders.
What are you hanging about for?

MERLIN.   I pluck at my roots
But they won't be fetched away from a world which possesses me
Like an unforgettable woman who was once my own.
I walk on the earth, besotted by her, waiting
To bring to her the devotion of my dust.

HOEL.   It's Merlin. He's still among us.

CYMEN.   What is he?
Is it one of your superstitions,
A damned invention of the air? Tell me
What your existence is or, by the night,
I'll ask your flesh with a sharper edge to the question.
Come on, now; are you superannuated god
Or working devil, or mere entangled man?

MERLIN. No god, I hope; that would take too much
Endurance. Whatever man may be
I am that thing, though my birth, I've been given to believe,
Had some darkness in it. But then, which of us
Can say he is altogether free of a strain
Of hell in his blood? My father could be called
Pure man, if such a thing existed.

CYMEN.   Then
What powers pursue us here? You know this island
Thoroughly. Parade your spirits, good
And bad, and I'll identify the mischief!

[125]

CLODESUIDA Will you ask *them*, men of the race
  We conquered?

MARTINA.   Ask the prisoner
  If he isn't a Christian. He's a godless Christian
  Even if he can't remember.

CLODESUIDA.   Why can't we get rid of them
  Once and for all? The gods will strike at them
  And everyone knows how carelessly they aim. The blow
  May fall on us.

COLGRIN.   Colgrin will catch it, Colgrin
  Is sure to catch it. The rest of the world will dodge
  And I shall be in the way.

CYMEN.   I'll ask the louse
  In the filthy shirt of a corpse in the bottom of a ditch
  If I can learn what it is I've learnt to dread.
  I lay on my bed and felt it stand with its feet
  Planted on either side of my heart, and I looked
  Up the tower of its body to find the face
  To know if it meant to help or hinder,
  But it was blotted out by a shield of thunder.
  Am I to sacrifice without end and then
  Be given no peace? The skirts of the gods
  Drag in our mud. We feel the touch
  And take it to be a kiss. But they see we soil them
  And twitch themselves away Name to me
  What mocked me with a mood of mercy and therefore
  Defeat. Who desired that?

MERLIN.   Who, apart
  From ourselves, can see any difference between
  Our victories and our defeats, dear sir?
  Not beast, nor bird, nor even the anticipating
  Vulture watching for the battle's end,

[126]

Nor a single mile of devoted dispassionate ground.
All indifferent. Much more so your gods
Who live without the world, who never feel
As the world feels in springtime the stab of the spear
And the spurt of golden blood,
Winter's wound-in-the-side, the place where life begins.
Nothing, it seems, cares for your defeat.

CLODESUIDA. How did I say these Britons would answer you?
It shames us to stand and listen. Didn't we conquer them?

MERLIN. Quest and conquest and quest again. It might well
Make you fretful if you weren't expecting it.

CYMEN. You are conquered. Both you or this boy
I can destroy now, and no questions asked.

MERLIN. Death is what conquers the killer, not the killed.
How pleasant it is to talk, even
In your language. I have a way—your daughter
May have told you—of looking ahead, having made
My peace with Time, at some expense to my soul.
It's curious to know that in the course
Of the movement of years which wears away distinction,
You, and moreover your conquerors, will bear
Kindly and as though by nature our name, the British
Name, and all the paraphernalia, legend
And history, as though you were our widow
Not our conqueror. And well may the weeds become you.

CYMEN. You're a hideous old wiseacre
Of sheepbitten kale. But give me an answer.
If, as you imagine, our gods have no care
Whether we win or lose, what cuckoo power
Is it that usurps the nest of my soul?

MERLIN. You ask an old pagan? Old Merlin, old
Eternal suckling, who cannot drag his lips

[127]

Away from the breast of the earth, even to grow
Into the maturity of heaven. Nothing can wean him
Until his mother puts upon her nipple
The vinegar of death, though, when I walked
Between the dog-rose hedges of my manhood,
It was in a Christian land: in Arthur's land.
There I gleamed in the iris of creation's
Eye, and there I laughed as a man should,
Between the pillars of my ribs in the wide
Nave of my chest. A Christian land. There
It was, and old Joseph's faithful staff
Breaking into scarlet bud in the falling snow.
But, as I said at the time, the miracle
Was commonplace: staves of chestnut wood
And maywood and the like perform it every year.
And men broke their swords in the love of battle,
And broke their hearts in the love of women,
And broke the holy bread in the love of God.
I saw them ride away between their loves
Into a circle of the snow-white wind
And so into my head's old yellow world
Of bone.

CYMEN.   Your Christian land was weak, it shook
Down, it burnt, its ash was blown
Into our food and drink. What I'm inflicted with
Is strong, destroying me with a cry of love,
A violence of humility arrogantly
Demanding all I am or possess or have ambitions for,
Insistent as a tocsin which was sounded
When the sun first caught on fire, and ever since
Clangs alarm with a steady beat in the wild
Night of history. This doesn't come

[128]

From the watery light of what you think you remember.
A lashing logic drags me away from my gods.
Let it face me like a man!

MERLIN.   It may be already
This power has faced you like a man, on a certain
Century's peak from which the circling low land
Is, to eternity, surveyed. Still, still,
Earth winds delicious arms; it isn't strange
Our human eyes should close upon her, like a flower
Closing on a globe of dew, and wish to see
Nothing but this. And here am I
Doting into oblivion.

CLODESUIDA.   Send him off,
With his ancient ramifications; go to sleep
And be well.

CYMEN [*to* HOEL]. Do I have to come to you again?
You, a speck of the dust which three of our generations
Have marched over: what light flung from you
To me? Why did my strength startle from your
Futility?

HOEL.   On my soul, I've done nothing against you
Except to make war. I've known nothing except
Your mercy; that indeed was a kind of light to me.
I want to live, having a life in me
Which seems to demand it.

MERLIN.   Having a death in him, too:
That death by drowning in the river of his baptism
From which he rose a dripping Christian child
In a land which had become a grave to us all,
Though in that grave of Britain old Merlin, for one,
Was happy enough because he could hold, both hill

[129]

And valley, his leafy love in his arms,
Old pagan that he is.

HOEL. The weather of twenty
Years has blown me dry, and long lost me
All the charms I ever had of that.

MERLIN. The spirit is very tenacious of such water.

CYMEN. The spirit again! You nod and look beyond me,
And pretend to know nothing. Do you dare to say
The world has a secret direction passing the gods?
And does it run through me? [*To* CLODESUIDA.] Take me from
    them.
I'm mad, mad to talk to the slaves.

CLODESUIDA. Rest, Cymen.

CYMEN. I am alive and so there is no rest.

CLODESUIDA. It's you who churn up the air; the air itself
Is as unruffled as ever. Trust our gods
And put these heathen to work.

Enter ANNA.

ANNA. Master, master, master!
Where is the master? The wolves, the savages!
An old woman's no use! Oh, the master!

CYMEN. What's the matter?

ANNA. So many wolves, the fields
Are a bear-garden—ma'am, your brothers!—grey,
Snarling, vicious, a terrible pack—they're into
The sheep!

CYMEN. The sheep!

CLODESUIDA. Brothers, help, help us,
Wake, the wolves have come!

[130]

ANNA.   The sheep and the lambs,
   All we have!

MARTINA.   In the daylight, in daylight, too!
   What could have brought them?

ANNA.   Why, hunger, hunger, the appetite,
   The spite of the belly!

        Enter TADFRID, OSMER, QUICHELM, *and* CHELDRIC.

OSMER.   What's the cry?

CLODESUIDA.   The wolves!
   They're falling on the flock!

TADFRID.   So it begins,
   Bad-luck already.

OSMER.   Down to them, then, and save
   What's still for saving.
              [CYMEN *has already snatched* COLGRIN'S *sword and gone;*
              HOEL *also, ahead of him. Now the rest follow, shouting to*
              scatter the wolves.

ANNA.   I'm fit for nothing now
   But whisking eggs, I'm trembling so.
   Why should such things be? Such fangs, I have
   Sharp pains in the back just to have seen them
   Gnashing in the light. [*Seeing* COLGRIN]: Why are you here,
   You, taking up space as though time didn't begin
   Until the day after to-morrow? Do all legs move
   Except the two that keep the ground away from you?
   Why don't you go and help?

COLGRIN.   My dear, good woman,
   I'm here on duty.

ANNA.   What duty would you mean,
   I wonder? The prisoner's gone.

                         [131]

COLGRIN.   All the more reason
   Why the other half of the arrangement should stand.
   If the horse gets out of the stable it doesn't mean
   The stable is justified in following.
   I'm a man who can be relied on.

ANNA.   So you are.
   Well, at least when your time comes to be buried
   They'll have no trouble keeping you under the ground.
   But why should wolves be set upon us? Men
   Make enough misfortunes for themselves, without
   Natural calamities happening as well.
   The old gentleman agrees.

MERLIN.   Considerable
   Age makes me nod; I neither agree
   Nor disagree. I'm too near-sighted now
   To be able to distinguish one thing from another,
   The storm-swollen river from the tear-swollen eyes,
   Or the bare cracked earth from the burnt-out face,
   Or the forest soughing from the sighing heart.
   What is in one is in the other, a mood
   Of rage which turns upon itself to savage
   Its own body, since there's nothing except itself
   On which anger can alight; it sinks into time
   Like a sword into snow
   And the roots receive all weathers and subsist,
   And the seasons are reconciled. When, years ago,
   The Romans fell away from our branching roads
   Like brazen leaves, answering
   The hopeless windy trumpets from their home,
   Your tribes waged winter upon us, till our limbs
   Ached with the carving cold. You blackened
   The veins of the valleys with our dried blood. And at last

Your lives croaked like crows on a dead bough
And the echoes clanged against you. But I can hear
Faintly on the twittering sea a sail
Moving greatly where the waves, like harvest-home,
Come hugely on our coast: the men of Rome
Returning, bringing God, winter over, a breath
Of green exhaled from the hedges, the wall of sky
Breached by larksong. Primrose and violet
And all frail privileges of the early ground
Gather like pilgrims in the aisles of the sun.
A ship in full foliage rides in
Over the February foam, and rests
Upon Britain.

COLGRIN.   He's in the clouds, you see; he's away
On his own; he's blowing about like the hairs in his beard.

ANNA. Maybe, yes, and maybe also his beard
Has caught on something. He seems to have brought
The other side of the hill into his head.
It's good to see—we anticipate little enough—
And certainly to-day, I noticed myself,
Winter is wearing thin; it's beginning to show
The flowering body through.

COLGRIN.   It's a hard time,
The spring; it makes me lose all my energy.

Enter CLODESUIDA.

CLODESUIDA. Did you see it, did ever your eyes? He must be as
    wild
As an animal in his heart! Who ever saw
Such wrestling between hand and claw?

ANNA.   Such what,
Such wrestling? I hadn't hard enough eyes

[133]

To put them again on those poor bleating lambs.
Are the wolves away now? Are the wolves away?
I still shake for the sake of those sheep.

CLODESUIDA.   The wolves
Are beaten off. But the Briton killed the grimmest,
The greatest: with his hands, with his hands as bare
As mine: met and mauled the scavenger, with a grip
Under the blood and froth of the jaws, he shook
And choked the howling out of its fangs
And forced it to a carcase. It was horror
And hope and terror and triumph to see it.

ANNA. The boy? The Briton? with bare hands?

MERLIN.   Like a shepherd
With a lion.

COLGRIN. With his bare hands?

ANNA.   It's just as well
To hang the wet linen on your sword,
You heavy hero on my conscience.

  Enter TADFRID, OSMER, QUICHELM, *and* CHELDRIC.

CLODESUIDA.   It's a tale
I'll tell to my grave! My heart is hammering
And still hugging the fearful sport of the struggle.
What shall we do to reward him?

OSMER.   Reward him? his death
Can reward him. Who's the fool who's going to kiss
Future trouble? Who does, deserves to lie
With the grass growing up through a crack in the skull.

CLODESUIDA. What do you mean? Didn't he enlist himself
Against our disaster?

TADFRID.   But in what power's name?
Osmer fears—

[134]

OSMER.   And very properly fears.
I'm not quite a child in this cleft-stick of life.

Enter CYMEN.

CYMEN. Are you still rolling your marbles of thunder?
I hear what you say. Still breaking wind to make
A hurricane. I am very tired.

OSMER.   And so
Are we all with anxiety. And so no doubt
Are the crouching gods who contain their final leap
Waiting for wisdom from us.

TADFRID.   And not holding
For long, now that the first roar has come.

CYMEN. That may be. I know well enough
The weight of the silence that's on our shoulders now.
I move under it like the moving mole
That raises the hackles of dead leaves.
Under me, silence; round me, silence, air,
The wind hushing the world to hear
The wind hushing the world; and over me,
Silence upon silence upon silence,
Unuttering vapour, unutterable void.
What do you want me to do?

OSMER.   Make retribution
Before we're godsmitten again.

TADFRID.   A sacrifice.

OSMER. The only possible sacrifice, the Briton.

CLODESUIDA. Can they be right, Cymen? Certainly
We must do what is necessary, though when
I saw the wolf destroyed—

OSMER.   As now you shall see
Our luck's neck fractured, unless we act.

[135]

The Briton sprang on the back of a punishment
Justly put upon us by the gods.

TADFRID. That's so. And by what muscle, except a devil's,
Could he elbow himself between our gods and us?

OSMER. It's perfectly proper that we should contest our punish-
ment,
If we can. The gods relish a knock or two
Before they lean back and insist on being
Propitiated. But by no right does this Briton
Break in and ruffle them beyond all hope.
His demon rams him to it to make our world
The worse for us.

QUICHELM.   We've got to be free of him.
Cut him to quiet. He's a flint that's going to skag us.
Hit the spark of life out of him, father.

TADFRID. What else but a power of the dark would send him
Scudding into the teeth and talons
Of a probable death, for us, his enemies?
If you let him live among us—

          [*Enter* HOEL, *helped by* MARTINA. *His shoulders have been
          clawed by the wolf. They walk across to the barn, watched in
          silence by the others.*

CYMEN.   I will sacrifice.

OSMER. Then back we come to easy breathing
And a chance of pleasure.

CLODESUIDA.   Let me think of the harm
He would do us, his brain's blackened teeth,
And not sicken at his killing. What the gods
Want we'll give them, even though our blood
Freezes.

[136]

CYMEN. I will sacrifice.
I'll pay off whatever dark debts there are
And come to the morning, square. I am tired, tired
Of being ground between the staring stones
Of air and earth. I'll satisfy the silence.
Bring me one of the white goats.

TADFRID *and* OSMER.   A goat?

CYMEN. One silence of death is as deep as another
To satisfy the silence. It will do
To patch wherever a whisper from above
Can still creep out. Bring me the goat.

CLODESUIDA.   But this
Can't please them if they demand the Briton?

OSMER. It's livestock thrown away.

TADFRID.   Look, he goes
To pray to them.

CYMEN [*at the altar*]. Gods, our gods, gods
Of the long forced-march of our blood's generations
Dead and living. Goaders, grappling gods,
Whose iron feet pace on thunder's floor
Up and down in the hall where chaos groaned
And bore creation sobbing. Boding gods,
Who broad in the universe consume our days
Like food, and crunch us, good and bad,
Like bones. What do I do by sacrifice?
The blood flows, the ground soaks it up,
The poisoned nightshade grows, the fears go on,
The dread of doom gropes into the bowels,
And hope, with her ambitious shovel, sweats
To dig the pit which swallows us at last.
The sacrifice is despair and desperation!

[137]

The deed of death is done and done and always
To do, death and death and death; and still
We cannot come and stand between your knees.
Why? By what stroke was the human flesh
Hacked so separate from the body of life
Beyond us? You make us to be the eternal alien
In our own world. Then I submit. Separation
To separation! Dedicated stones
Can lie asunder until the break is joined!

> [CYMEN *throws down the stones of the altar. The rest, except*
> HOEL, *throw themselves in horror on to the ground.*

Answer, then, answer! I am alone, without hope.
The outlaw, no longer the groveller on the knee.
Silence me! Come down and silence me!
Then at least I shall have some kind of part
With all the rest.

> [*They wait.*]
> Not even that?

Is separation between man and gods
So complete? Can't you even bring me to silence?

> [*A voice from a short way off is heard calling 'Cymen!*
> *Cymen of the Copse!'* CYMEN *stands startled. The rest raise*
> *themselves partly from the ground in apprehension. The voice*
> *calls, again, nearer.*

CYMEN. What is it? Who is it? I am here on my ground.

Enter a MESSENGER.

MESSENGER. Cymen of the Copse, is he here?

CYMEN.   I'm that man.

MESSENGER. You're summoned to the general assemblage
Of all householders, copyholders, smallholders, and tenant-
    farmers,
At the command of Ethelbert, lord and king of Kent,

To receive the person and words of Augustine
Exponent of the Christian god.
Proper precautions are being taken, and all
Provision made, to protect each person present
From being taken at a disadvantage
By the craft of any spirit whatsoever,
Evil or good. Therefore you will take your stand
Not under the king's roof
But where the air keeps open house
And the sun in the sky suffers all for all,
Or at least if any charms are set afoot
They will be less concentrated, owing to the wind.

CYMEN. Am I called to the king?

MESSENGER.   You assemble on the western hill
To receive the person and words—

MERLIN.   Of Augustine
Sent by Gregory of Rome who on a market-day
Saw angels where we see our enemies.

ANNA. He knew, that's what he said, he saw them coming
In a ship full of primroses from Rome!

CYMEN [to the MESSENGER]. I am slow to understand you. I was
  up
On the bare back of dreadful thoughts. Who chose
That you should come to me now? What ground
Am I dismounting onto, your ordinary summons
To the king?

MESSENGER. You find it unpleasant? The news, I see,
Has reached you already, and distaste, I suppose,
Is understandable, though all you're supposed to do
Is to sit and give the appearance of paying attention
Out of consideration for the queen.

[139]

CLODESUIDA. She would like to make heathen of us all!
We're on poor enough terms with the gods as it is
Without seeming to keep open minds.

OSMER.   They're only
Hesitating over the choice of weapons
They mean to use against us.

TADFRID.   The sky is clear,
The sun still shines, but there's little doubt
Their indignation is mounting under the self-control
Of the horizon. Let the king indulge the queen
If it keeps her wife-minded, but here more than ever
We've got to remain rigid with reality.

MESSENGER. In my opinion you're taking devoutness too hard.
The gods won't object to our being a bit diplomatic.
I'll leave you to make your way, Cymen of the Copse.

CYMEN. Time makes my way, and I go on with time.
What is contrives what will be. Yes, I shall come.

[*Exit the* MESSENGER.

TADFRID. Will you go and leave us now to suffer
In whatever suffering comes of your blasphemy?

OSMER. Let him go.

CLODESUIDA.   But now of all times isn't the time;
He's so wretched from his brainstorm of wrong,
Every pore of his skin's wide open to punishment.

OSMER. Let him go, let him go.

CYMEN [*to* HOEL].   Your god has come, perhaps,
Or lies in wait on the lips of a man from Rome.
Strange. As though a spirit in you, like
A wild fowl hiding in the mere of your flesh,
Heard the sound far off and flew up clamouring
Rousing a spirit in me. We're in the path

[140]

Of change. And I must go to meet the change,
Being unable to live unaltered.

HOEL.   Is it true,
Indeed? Is the One god making his way again
In through the many?

CYMEN.   I go to know.
I go to dare my arm into the thicket
To know what lifts its head there, whether rose
Or tiger, or tiger and rose together.
Be undisturbed, my dear disturbed wife.
If I rock, it's with the rocking of the world;
It will get me to sleep in time. As for the rest of you,
Wait, with a certain degree of trust.
Yes, you can build up the altar again if you must.
It will be somewhere to sit when the days are warmer.
Meanwhile, the silence keep you, the silence
Be gracious unto you and give you peace.

> [*Exit* CYMEN. TADFRID *and* OSMER *have started, and now*
> *continue, to rebuild the altar.* CLODESUIDA *watches* CYMEN
> *on his way.*

CLODESUIDA. Should he go? He walks steadily enough now,
Very much as he does behind a plough. Is this only
A lull on his brain? Can he avoid trouble
After what he has done?

TADFRID.   The air is clearer without him.
And let's hope the bloodshot eyes above us
Have followed him and don't still fix on us here.

QUICHELM. It was awful to watch him. We must make it right with
      the gods.
They can't expect sons to carry the blame for fathers.
Would they make us suffer because of our blood?

HOEL.   Yes;
   Or from whose example would men have learnt that trick?

OSMER. You'll scream yourself sorry if we turn ourselves to you.

MARTINA [*to* HOEL]. You're still a Briton, even though I have
   Washed your wounds. Lie low, and don't make trouble.

CHELDRIC. Our mother's blood flows in us too, uncle,
   And mother fears the gods. Won't that be taken
   Into account?

CLODESUIDA. The same with the gods as with men;
   Women are only camp-followers, they take
   Our obedience for granted. If *we* blasphemed
   They would pinch our cheeks and resume the course of history
   As though nothing had happened. We succeed or suffer
   According to our men.

ANNA.   Then I roughen my hands
   For a fine lark.

CLODESUIDA. Day's work is still to do,
   Whatever the day's doom. I have no hope
   To be able to know what hope to have. My hands
   Can only draw their everyday conclusions.

ANNA. Yes, we must busy ourselves, and try to forget
   The complication of what's up there beyond us.
   [*To* COLGRIN.] Are you still rooted to the spot with duty?

COLGRIN. Unavoidably static.

OSMER.   Get onto your work.

COLGRIN. But suppose the prisoner—

OSMER.   Suppose
   You do what you're told and quick.

COLGRIN.   Quick? I'll suppose
   Anything once; but that's not how I am.
   I was born midway between the quick and the dead.

[142]

ANNA. Budge over a little farther from the grave.
[*Exeunt* CLODESUIDA, COLGRIN, *and* ANNA.

TADFRID. What do we mean to do? The altar stones
Now stand as they were. But not to them.
To them the stones are still pitching and blundering
From jutting god to jutting god, down
The scowling scarp of their everlasting memory.
They say the gods were formed
Out of the old hurt pride of rejected chaos
Which is still lusting for the body of the world we walk on.

OSMER. If they'll give us time and the merest shove
In the lucky direction we're leaning to already,
We shall be able to elude the allegiance to Cymen
Which is such an obstacle in the way of well-doing,
Nullify guilt and mollify the gods
And bury the brat's guts for good in the ground.
You shall see; it will be as I say
If the gods give us time.

TADFRID.   But Cymen claimed
His death to himself.

OSMER.   We'll do it in his name;
If a moment which insists on action
Comes while he's away, he would expect us
To live the moment for him.

TADFRID.   If the crisis came.

QUICHELM. What's the talk? Do you think we're in for the worst?
Do you see any hope that we can relax
Now that father's gone, or what's your guess?

CHELDRIC. Isn't the danger less?

OSMER.   Come away from here.
I've got a screw of courage you can chew;

We're not committed to damnation yet.
Let your sister stay. We'll pray, with a certain purpose.

[*Exeunt* TADFRID, OSMER, QUICHELM, *and* CHELDRIC.

MARTINA. They hate you; and that's easy to understand.
We have existence on such hard terms,
As though birth into the world had been a favour
Instantly regretted. We haven't the air
To spare for strangers. I hope the claw-marks heal.
I've done my best for them.

HOEL.   Thanks. Are you going in?

MARTINA. Of course. There's nothing to keep me here.

HOEL. No; there's nothing.

MARTINA.   What do you want?

HOEL.   I wonder
What it was that came and wielded your father and left me
Alive?

MARTINA. I'll not worry about my father,
Nor my mother, nor my uncles nor, between ourselves,
The gods. The universe is too ill-fitting
And large. I am very careful about small
Things, such as wearing green in the third month
Or bringing blackthorn under the roof;
But the big things, such as gods, must look after themselves.

HOEL. Still, I'm curious about the One god.
I've never completely shaken him off. He seems
To insist.

MARTINA. You're a born heathen. Get some sleep.
You look too tired to be hated
And that won't do at all.

HOEL.   Do you have to hate me?

[144]

MARTINA. It isn't one of my easiest duties. But how else
  Can we keep our footing or our self-esteem?
  Now sleep and look malignant when you wake.

HOEL. Sleep, yes. My fields need rain. Sleep
  Can drench down and welcome.
               [*Exit* MARTINA. HOEL *lies in the straw and sleeps.*

MERLIN.   Welcome, sleep;
  Welcome into the winter head of the world
  The sleep of Spring, which grows dreams,
  Nodding trumpets, blowing bells,
  A jingle of birds whenever the sun moves,
  Never so lightly; all dreams,
  All dreams out of slumbering rock:
  Lambs in a skittle prance, the hobbling rook
  Like a witch picking sticks,
  And pinnacle-ears the hare
  Ladling himself along in the emerald wheat:
  All dreams out of the slumbering rock,
  Each dream answering to a shape
  Which was in dream before the shapes were shapen;
  Each growing obediently to a form,
  To its own sound, shrill or deep, to a life
  In water or air, in light or night or mould;
  By sense or thread perceiving,
  Eye, tendril, nostril, ear; to the shape of the dream
  In the ancient slumbering rock.
  And above the shapes of life, the shape
  Of death, the singular shape of the dream dissolving,
  Into which all obediently come.
  And above the shape of death, the shape of the will
  Of the slumbering rock, the end of the throes of sleep
  Where the stream of the dream wakes in the open eyes

Of the sea of the love of the morning of the God.
Here's an old man whiling away a spring
Day, with thoughts so far beyond the moss
He roots in, they're as nebulous
As the muted flute of a dove to the root of a tree.
Never mind. However warmly I curl
My tail around my feet and admire myself
Reflected in the nut before I bite,
Still I observe the very obdurate pressure
Edging men towards a shape beyond
The shape they know. Now and then, by a spurt
Of light, they manage the clumsy approximation,
Overturn it, turn again, refashion
Nearer the advising of their need.
Always the shape lying over the life.
Pattern of worm in the sand was not the shape,
Nor the booming body of enormous beast,
Nor the spread fan of the blue-eyed quivering tail,
Nor the weave of the nest, nor the spun wheel of the web,
Nor the maze and cellarage of honey, nor
The charts and maps of men. The shape shone
Like a faint circle round a moon
Of hazy gods, and age by age
The gods reformed according to the shape,
According to the shape that was a word,
According to Thy Word. Here's more than half
A pagan whiling away the spring sunshine.
The morning has come within a distant sight
Of evening, and the wandering shadows begin
To stretch their limbs a little. I shall move
Myself, into the quiet of the tumbling tower,
For an hour or two of casual obliteration
And break more ground for dreams.

[*Exit* MERLIN. *Enter, after a pause,* MARTINA *with a bowl
of food. She goes to* HOEL, *who is still asleep.*

MARTINA. You're even less of an enemy when you sleep.
Wake up. You've gone where we're all of one size.
Bring yourself back and know your station.

HOEL.   Yes?
This isn't where I sleep. Why is my heart
So heavy?

MARTINA. Here is food. You have to be
A good enemy and eat.

HOEL.   You went indoors.
I thought you might not come back again.

MARTINA. Aren't you hungry?

HOEL.   Perhaps. From where I sit
On the kerb of sleep I feel I know you better
Than I did before. Take the bowl in your hands
And let me eat the food from there.

MARTINA. Am I your servant?

HOEL.   I'm your servant. I slept
When you said sleep, and I'll eat like a tame swan
Out of your hands.

MARTINA.   Too black for a swan,
You'd make me a good shadow. I'll ask my father
To give you to be my personal shadow,
To walk behind me in the morning, and before me
In the evening, and at noon I'll have you
Under my feet.

HOEL.   I shall adjust myself
Easily to noon.

MARTINA.   You'll feel humiliated
And bite the dust.

HOEL.   I shall feel delighted
And kiss the sole of your foot.

MARTINA.   It's clear you're nothing
But a poor-spirited Briton if you're willing
To become a girl's shadow.

HOEL.   Yes, indeed;
A poor-spirited Briton; you remind me
In good time.

MARTINA.   But a Briton who, if he were a Jute,
Would be brave and agreeable. So be glad of that.

HOEL. What simple-witted things the affections are,
That can't perceive whether people are enemies
Or friends. You would think the strong distinction
Between race and race would be clear even to the heart
Though it does lie so retired
Beating its time away in the human breast.

MARTINA. You talk of nothing that interests me. Eat
Your food.

        Enter TADFRID, OSMER, QUICHELM, *and* CHELDRIC.

OSMER.   You see, she has gone to him again.
It's the way I said it would be. His damned contagion
Spreads.

TADFRID. It flies first to the weakest place.
That girl sees nothing but an eye and a mouth
And doesn't care.

QUICHELM.   She can go and eat grass
Before I call her sister again.

OSMER.   She gives us
The grounds for getting him where the gods want him.
He is ours and his blood's as good as gone to them.

[148]

If we hesitated now even Cymen would say
We were as puny as pulp.

MARTINA [*to* HOEL].   You look so sad.
       [*She kisses him on the forehead.*

QUICHELM [*leaping forward*]. Leper-flesh!

CHELDRIC.   He snared her!

MARTINA.   What's so wrong?

QUICHELM. You and the flicker of your rutting eyes are wrong!

OSMER. Toleration has gone to the limit. Now
We strike. You black pawn of the devil's game,
Come out.

HOEL.   Why, what is it you mean to do?

OSMER. Make much of you, make a god's meal of you,
And make our peace with you, with you as peacemaker,
And not too soon. It's a quiet future for you.
I said come out.

MARTINA.   No! My father said he was not to be harmed!

OSMER. He wouldn't say it now. Uncertainty
Has dandled us enough to make us sick
For life. Now we're not going to fob
The gods off any longer.

QUICHELM.   Must we wait?
Give me the word, and I'll fetch his cringing carcase
Out for you.

MARTINA.   Don't dare to touch him!

TADFRID.   Niece,
We must submit to the wish of what we worship.
We rid the world of an evil. Let's not rage.
We do what's demanded of us, with solemnity,
Without passion. Fetch him out.

[149]

MARTINA.   No, you shall not!

OSMER. Take her!

> [CHELDRIC *drags back* MARTINA *and holds her.* OSMER
> *and* QUICHELM *fetch* HOEL *to the centre of the stage.*

MARTINA.   Cowards!

HOEL.   Let me live, do, do
Let me live.

TADFRID. Bring him to the tree; we'll offer him
In Woden's way, the Woden death. Come on;
We'll be well out of our fear.

MARTINA.   Cowards, cowards,
Cowards, sneakthieves, only dare with father gone!

> [*They fasten him to the tree with his arms spread.*

HOEL. Is this the end indeed? Where now for me?

MARTINA. Father! Father!

HOEL.   Son and the brooding dove.
Call him again.

MARTINA.   Father!

OSMER.   We set this house
Free from fear and guilt and the working of darkness.

QUICHELM. We clean our hearts.

TADFRID.   The sun flows on the spear.
The spear answers the sun. They are one, and go
To the act in the concord of a sacrifice.

HOEL. Death, be to me like a hand that shades
My eyes, helping me to see
Into the light.

[150]

OSMER. Woden, we pay your dues
  Of blood.

TADFRID. Receive it and receive us back
  Into a comfortable security.
      [OSMER *makes to plunge the spear.* MARTINA *breaks free of*
      CHELDRIC *and crying 'No!' tries to prevent the stroke,*
      [*Enter* CLODESUIDA.

CLODESUIDA. Have they struck at us again, the gods?
  What more
  Have we to bear?

MARTINA.   Look, look!

CLODESUIDA [*covering her eyes*]. It has to be
  For our good; we must endure these things, to destroy
  Error, and so the gods will warm towards us.

QUICHELM. Here comes my father home!

OSMER.   Well, home he comes.
  We're in the right.

TADFRID.   He will understand this tree
  By reason of our plight had to bear such fruit.
      [*Enter* CYMEN. *He goes towards the barn, near which*
      CLODESUIDA *is now standing.*

CYMEN. Clodesuida, a peaceful heart to you now.
  I am well; I have seen our terrible gods come down
  To beg the crumbs which fall from our sins, their only
  Means of life. This evening you and I
  Can walk under the trees and be ourselves
  Together, knowing that this wild day has gone
  For good. Where is the Briton? You still think
  You must be afraid and see in him
  The seed of a storm. But I have heard

[151]

Word of his God, and felt our lonely flesh
Welcome to creation. The fearful silence
Became the silence of great sympathy,
The quiet of God and man in the mutual word.
And never again need we sacrifice, on and on
And on, greedy of the gods' goodwill
But always uncertain; for sacrifice
Can only perfectly be made by God
And sacrifice has so been made, by God
To God in the body of God with man,
On a tree set up at the four crossing roads
Of earth, heaven, time, and eternity
Which meet upon that cross. I have heard this;
And while we listened, with our eyes half-shut
Facing the late sun, above the shoulder
Of the speaking man I saw the cross-road tree,
The love of the God hung on the motes and beams
Of light, as though—

MARTINA.   Father!

                    [CYMEN *turns and sees* HOEL.

CYMEN.   Is it also here?
Can the sun have written it so hotly on to my eyes—
What have you done?

OSMER.   The unavoidable moment
Came while you were gone—

CYMEN.   What have you done?

TADFRID. Would *you* not break the body of our evil?

CYMEN. I will tell you what I know. Cut him down.
O pain of the world!—I will tell you what I know.
Bring him here to me.

CLODESUIDA.   We have to live.

[152]

CYMEN. We have still to learn to live.

[*They bring* HOEL *to* CYMEN.

They say
The sacrifice of God was brought about
By the blind anger of men, and yet God made
Their blindness their own saving and lonely flesh
Welcome to creation. Briton, boy,
Your God is here, waiting in this land again.
Forgive me for the sorrow of this world.

MARTINA. You haven't made the sorrow—

CYMEN.   All make all:
For while I leave one muscle of my strength
Undisturbed, or hug one coin of ease
Or private peace while the huge debt of pain
Mounts over all the earth,
Or, fearing for myself, take half a stride
Where I could leap; while any hour remains
Indifferent, I have no right or reason
To raise a cry against this blundering cruelty
Of man.

OSMER. Shall we let the light of our lives
Be choked by darkness?

CYMEN.   Osmer,
What shall we do? We are afraid
To live by rule of God, which is forgiveness,
Mercy, and compassion, fearing that by these
We shall be ended. And yet if we could bear
These three through dread and terror and terror's doubt,
Daring to return good for evil without thought
Of what will come, I cannot think
We should be the losers. Do we believe
There is no strength in good or power in God?

[153]

God give us courage to exist in God,
And lonely flesh be welcome to creation.
Carry him in.

> [*As they carry* HOEL *away*, CYMEN, CLODESUIDA, *and*
> MARTINA *following, the voices of Augustine's men are heard
> singing.*

THE END

A SLEEP OF PRISONERS

To

ROBERT GITTINGS

Dear Robert

 It is nineteen years this summer since you persuaded me to take a holiday from my full-time failure to make a living, and sat me down, with a typewriter and a barrel of beer, in the empty rectory at Thorn St. Margaret. I had written almost nothing for five or six years, and I was to write almost nothing again for five years following, but the two months we spent at Thorn, two months (it seems to me now) of continuous blazing sunshine, increased in me the hope that one day the words would come. It was all very well that I should look obstinately forward to plays which I showed no sign of writing. It was an extraordinary faith which made you also look obstinately forward to them. The ten years in which you loyally thought of me as a writer when clearly I wasn't, your lectures to me on my self-defensive mockery of artists, and those two leisure months under the Quantocks, were things of friendship which kept me in a proper mind.

 We were talking even then, as we are talking, with greater instancy, now, of the likelihood of war. And I think we realized then, as we certainly now believe, that progress is the growth of vision: the increased perception of what makes for life and what makes for death. I have tried, as you know, not altogether successfully, to find a way for comedy to say something of this, since comedy is an essential part of men's understanding. In A Sleep of Prisoners *I have tried to make a more simple statement, though in a complicated design where each of four men is seen through the sleeping thoughts of the others, and each, in his own dream, speaks as at heart he is, not as he believes himself to be. In the later part of Corporal Adams' dream the dream changes to a state of thought entered into by all the sleeping men, as though, sharing their prison life, they shared, for a few moments of the night, their sleeping life also.*

A SLEEP OF PRISONERS

First performed in Oxford at the University Church on 23 April 1951 and in London at St. Thomas's Church, Regent Street, on 15 May 1951 with the following cast:

Private David King	LEONARD WHITE
Private Peter Able	DENHOLM ELLIOTT
Private Tim Meadows	HUGH PRYSE
Corporal Joe Adams	STANLEY BAKER

The play was produced by Michael MacOwan

CHARACTERS

PRIVATE DAVID KING

PRIVATE PETER ABLE

PRIVATE TIM MEADOWS

CORPORAL JOE ADAMS

The interior of a church, turned into a prison camp. One prisoner,
PETER ABLE, *is in the organ loft, playing 'Now the day is over'*
with one finger. Another, DAVID KING, *is looking at the memorial*
tablets on the wall. Four double bunks stand between the choir-
stalls. A pile of straw and a pile of empty paillasses are on the
chancel steps.

DAVID [*shouting up to the organ loft*]. Hey, Pete, come down and
tell me what this Latin
Says. If it's Latin.

PETER [*still playing*]. Why, what for?

DAVID. For the sake of that organ. And because I want to know
If 'Hic jacet' means what it looks like.

            [PETER *changes the tune to 'Three Blind Mice'.*
[*In a flash of temper.*]
And because I said so, that's what for, because
I said so! And because you're driving me potty.

PETER. Excuse me a minute: this is the difficult bit.

DAVID. If you want it difficult, go on playing. I swear
I'll come up there and put my foot through you.

      [*As the playing goes on* DAVID *suddenly howls like a dog and*
      starts tearing up a hymn-book.

PETER [*the playing over*]. It's the universal language, Dave. It's
music.

DAVID. Music my universal aunt. It's torture.
      [*He finds himself with a page or two of the hymn-book in his*
      hand.
Here, I know this one.
[*Sings.*] 'All things bright and beautiful——'

PETER [*coming down from the loft*]. That doesn't mean you, Davy.
Put it down.

DAVID. 'All creatures great and small—'
Well, one of those is me: I couldn't miss it.
'All things wise and wonderful——'

[CORPORAL JOE ADAMS *comes to the steps with more straw.*

ADAMS. Come and get it!

PETER. What is it? Soup?

ADAMS. Straw.

PETER. Never could digest it.

[TIM MEADOWS, *a middle-aged man—indeed he looks well
on towards sixty—limps up to the pile of straw.*

ADAMS. How's the leg feel, Meadows?

MEADOWS. Ah, all right.
I wouldn't be heard saying anything about one leg
I wouldn't say about the other.

PETER. Where
Did you get it, chum?

MEADOWS. I had it for my birthday.
Quite nice, isn't it? Five toes, it's got.

PETER. I mean where was the fighting, you wit?

MEADOWS [*jerking his head*]. Down the road.
My Uncle George had a thumping wooden leg,
Had it with him, on and off, for years.
When he gave up the world, it got out in the wash house.

DAVID. Has anybody thought what it's going to be like
Suppose we stay here for months or years?

ADAMS. Best they can do. You heard the towzer Commandant:
'All more buildings blow up into sky.
No place like home now. Roof here. Good and kind
To prisoners. Keep off sun, keep off rain.'

[162]

PETER. Keep off the grass.

DAVID. It's a festering idea for a prison can
You have to think twice every time you thi.
In case what you think's a bit on the dubiou
It's all this smell of cooped-up angels
Worries me.

PETER.   What, us?

DAVID.   Not mother's angels,
Dumb-cluck, God's angels.

_R.   Oh yes, them.
  're a worse fug to them, I shouldn't wonder.
  shall just have to make allowances.

DAVID.   Beg pardon:
  ʾn talking to no-complaints Pete: arrangements perfect.

  MS. Too many pricking thistles in this straw:
  icked to hell.

                    [PETER _has wandered across to the lectern._

PETER.   Note his early perpendicular
Language. Ecclesiastical influence.
See this? They've put us an English Bible.
There's careful nannies for you . . . 'These were the sons
Of Caleb the son of Hur, the firstborn of Ephratah:
Shobal the father of Kirjath-jearim, Salma
The father of Beth-lehem, Hareph the father
Of Beth-gader. And Shobal the father of Kirjath-
Jearim had sons: Haroeh, and half of the Manahethites——'
Interesting, isn't it?

DAVID.   Stuff it, Pete.

PETER. 'And these were the sons of David, which were born unto
Him in Hebron: the firstborn Amnon, of Ahinoam the

[163]

zreelitess: the second Daniel, of Abigail the
armelitess: the third Absalom the son of Maacah the
Daughter of Talmai king of Geshur: the fourth Adonijah
The son of Haggith: the fifth Shephatiah of Abital:
The sixth Ithream by Eglah his wife . . .'

                                    Doing

    All right, aren't you, Davey?

DAVID. So I did in Sunday school. You know what Absalom
    Said to the tree? 'You're getting in my hair.'
    And that's what I mean, so shut up.

PETER.   Shut up we are.
    Don't mind me. I'm making myself at home.
    Now all I've got to do is try the pulpit.

ADAMS. Watch yourself, Pete. We've got years of this.

DAVID [*his temper growing*]. Any damn where he makes himself at
    home.
    The world blows up, there's Pete there in the festering
    Bomb-hole making cups of tea. I've had it
    Week after week till I'm sick. Don't let's mind
    What happens to anybody, don't let's object to anything,
    Let's give the dirty towzers a cigarette,
    There's nothing on earth worth getting warmed up about!
    It doesn't matter who's on top, make yourself at home.

ADAMS. Character of Private Peter Able:
    And not so far out at that. What we're in for
    We've got to be in for and know just what it is.
    Have some common sense, Pete. If you're looking for trouble
    Go and have it in the vestry.

PETER [*up in the pulpit*]. How can I help it if I can't work myself up
    About the way things go? It's a mystery to me.
    We've had all this before. For God's sake

Be reasonable, Dave. Perhaps I was meant
To be a bishop.
[*He turns to the nave.*] Dearly beloved brothers
In a general muck-up, towzers included . . .

DAVID. What the hell do you think we're stuck here for
Locked in like lunatics? Just for a nice
New experience, with nice new friends
With nice new rifles to look after us?
We're at war with them, aren't we? And if we are
They're no blaming use!

PETER [*continuing to preach*]. We have here on my left
An example of the bestial passions that beset mankind.

> [DAVID, *beside himself, leaps up the steps and attacks* PETER
> *in the pulpit.*

Davey, Dave . . . don't be a lunatic!

ADAMS.   Come out of it,
King. Come down here, you great tomfool!

> [*He goes to drag* DAVID *away.* DAVID *has his hands on*
> PETER'S *throat and has pushed him across the edge of the*
> *pulpit.*

DAVID [*raging*]. You laugh: I'll see you never laugh again.
Go on: laugh at this.

MEADOWS.   If you don't get your hands away
You'll wish you never had 'em. Give over! Give over!

> [DAVID *releases his hold. He pushes past* ADAMS *and comes*
> *down from the pulpit.*

I see the world in you very well. 'Tisn't
Your meaning, but you're a clumsy, wall-eyed bulldozer.
You don't know what you're hitting.

> [DAVID *goes past him without a word, and throws himself on*
> *to his bed.*

[165]

                                                 Ah, well,
Neither do I, of course, come to that.

ADAMS. All right, Peter?

PETER.   Think so, Corporal,
I'm not properly reassembled yet.
There's a bit of a rattle, but I think I had that before.

ADAMS. Dave had better damp down that filthy volcano
Or let me know what.

PETER.   Oh, lord, I don't know,
It's who we happen to be. I suppose I'd better
Hit him back some time, or else he'll go mad
Trying to make me see daylight. I don't know.
I'll tell you my difficulty, Corp. I never remember
I ought to be fighting until I'm practically dead.
Sort of absent-fisted. Very worrying for Dave.

> [*They have come down from the pulpit.* PETER *sways on his feet.* ADAMS *supports him.*

ADAMS. You're all in, Pete.

PETER.   Say 'Fall out' and watch me
Fall.

ADAMS. All right, come on, we'll put you to bed.

> [MEADOWS *has limped across with two blankets for* PETER'S *bunk.* DAVID *is watching anxiously.*

DAVID. What's wrong, Pete?

ADAMS.   The best thing for you is keep
Out of this.

PETER.   Dog-tired, that's all. It comes
Of taking orders. Dog collar too tight.

[166]

DAVID. I'll see to him.

ADAMS.   I've seen you see to him.
Get back on your bed.

DAVID.   I've never killed him yet.
I'm a pal of his.

ADAMS.   That's right. I couldn't have expressed it
Better myself. We'll talk about that tomorrow.

> [*He goes over to make up his own bunk.* DAVID *unlaces*
> PETER's *boots.*

DAVID. How d'you feel now, Pete?

PETER.   Beautiful.

DAVID.   Why don't
You do some slaughtering sometimes? Why always
Leave it to me? Got no blood you can heat
Up or something? I didn't hurt you, did I,
Pete? How d'you feel?

PETER [*almost asleep*]. Um? Fine.

DAVID [*taking off* PETER's *socks for him*]. The world's got to have
us. Things go wrong.
We've got to finish the dirty towzers. It's been
A festering day, and I'm stinking tired. See you
Tomorrow.

> [*He leaves* PETER *sleeping, goes over to his own bunk, and
> throws himself down.*

ADAMS [*to* MEADOWS]. I sometimes feel a bit like Dave
Myself, about Pete. You have to tell him there's a war on.

> [MEADOWS *has taken his boots and socks off and is lying on
> top of his blankets.*

[167]

MEADOWS. Sometimes I think if it wasn't for the words, Corporal,
  I should be very given to talking. There's things
  To be said which would surprise us if ever we said them.

ADAMS. Don't give us any more surprises, for God's sake.

MEADOWS. There's things would surprise us.

ADAMS [*studying the sole of his foot*]. Like the size of that blister.

MEADOWS. Or even bigger. Well, good night, Corporal.

ADAMS. G'night, boy.

MEADOWS.   I'm old enough to be
  Your father.

ADAMS.   I thought you might be. How did you get
  Pulled in on this?

MEADOWS.   I thought I would.
  I got in under the fence. Not a soul
  At the War Office had noticed me being born.
  I'd only my mother's word for it myself,
  And she never knew whether it was Monday washing-day
  Or Thursday baking-day. She only knew
  I made it hindering awkward.

ADAMS.   Are you glad
  You came?

MEADOWS.   Ah, now. Well,
  Glad, yes, and sorry, yes, and so as that.
  I remember how it came over me, as I
  Was dunging a marrow bed. Tim, I said to me—
  'Cos being a widower I do the old lady's
  Talking for her, since she fell silent—Tim,
  You're in the way to curse. Thinking of the enemy
  And so as that. And I cursed up and about.
  But cursing never made anything for a man yet.

[168]

So having had the pleasure of it, I came along
To take a hand. But there's strange divisions in us,
And in every man, one side or the other.
When I'm not too good I hear myself talking away
Like Tim Meadows M.P., at the other end of my head.
Sounds all right. I'd like to know what I say.
Might be interesting.

ADAMS.   I shouldn't worry.
I'm going to take a last look at Pete.
G'night, boy.

MEADOWS [*already almost asleep*]. Hope so.

                          [ADAMS *goes over to* PETER'S *bunk*.

DAVID.   Corp.

ADAMS. Hullo.

DAVID.   How long are we here for?

ADAMS.   A million years.
So you'd better get to like it.

DAVID.   Give us
Cassock and surplice drill tomorrow, Joe.

ADAMS. O.K. Wash your feet.

DAVID.   How's Pete? Asleep?

ADAMS. Couldn't be more if he died.

DAVID [*starting up on his elbow*].   What do you mean?

ADAMS. I mean he's breathing like an easy conscience. Why don't
    you
Get down to it yourself? There's tomorrow to come,
According to orders. Good night, King of Israel.

[169]

DAVID. Oh, go
And discard yourself. G'night, Corporal Joseph Adams.

[ADAMS *goes to his bunk.* MEADOWS *turns in his sleep. The church clock strikes a single note.*

MEADOWS [*asleep*]. Who's that, fallen out? How many men?
How many? I said only one.
One was enough.
No, no, no. I didn't ask to be God.
No one else prepared to spell the words.
Spellbound. B-o-u-n-d. Ah-h-h-h . . .

[*He turns in his sleep again.*

It's old Adam, old, old, old Adam.
Out of bounds. No one said fall out.
What time did you go to bad?
Sorrow, Adam, stremely sorrow.

[CORPORAL ADAMS *comes towards him, a dream figure.*

Adam, Adam, stand easy there.

ADAMS. Reporting for duty, sir.

MEADOWS. As you were, Adam.

ADAMS. No chance of that, sir.

MEADOWS. As you were, as you were.

ADAMS. Lost all track of it now, sir.

MEADOWS. How far back was it, Adam?

ADAMS [*with a jerk of the head*]. Down the road. Too dark to see.

MEADOWS. Were you alone?

ADAMS. A woman with me, sir.

MEADOWS. I said Let there be love,
And there wasn't enough light, you say?

ADAMS. We could see our own shapes, near enough,
But not the road. The road kept on dividing
Every yard or so. Makes it long.
We expected nothing like it, sir.
Ill-equipped, naked as the day,
It was all over and the world was on us
Before we had time to take cover.

MEADOWS. Stand at peace, Adam: do stand at peace.

ADAMS. There's nothing of that now, sir.

MEADOWS. Corporal Adam.

ADAMS.   Sir?

MEADOWS.   You have shown spirit.

ADAMS. Thank you, sir.
Excuse me, sir, but there's some talk of a future.
I've had no instructions.

MEADOWS [*turning in his sleep*]. Ah-h-h-h-h.

ADAMS. Is there any immediate anxiety of that?

[DAVID, *as the dream figure of Cain, stands leaning on the
lectern, chewing at a beet.*

How far can we fall back, sir?

DAVID [*smearing his arms with beet juice*]. Have you lost something?

ADAMS. Yes, Cain: yes, I have.

DAVID. Have you felt in all your pockets?

ADAMS. Yes, and by searchlight all along the grass
For God knows howling. Not a sign,
Not a sign, boy, not a ghost.

DAVID.   When do you last
Remember losing it?

ADAMS.   When I knew it was mine.
As soon as I knew it was mine I felt
I was the only one who didn't know
The host.

DAVID.   Poor overlooked
Old man. Allow me to make the introduction.
God: man. Man: God.

> [PETER, *the dream figure of Abel, is in the organ-loft finger-*
> *ing out 'Now the day is over'.*

ADAMS. I wish it could be so easy.

DAVID. Sigh, sigh, sigh!
The hot sun won't bring you out again
If you don't know how to behave.
Pretty much like mutiny. I'd like to remind you
We're first of all men, and complain afterwards.
[*Calling.*] Abel! Abel! Hey, flock-headed Peter,
Come down off those mountains.
Those bleating sheep can look after themselves.
Come on down.

PETER.   What for?

DAVID.   Because I said so!

PETER [*coming down*]. I overlooked the time. Is it day or night?

DAVID. You don't deserve to inherit the earth.
Am I supposed to carry the place alone?

PETER. Where will you carry it?
Where do you think you're going to take it to,
This prolific indifference?
Show me an ending great enough
To hold the passion of this beginning
And raise me to it.

[172]

Day and night, the sun and moon
Spirit us, we wonder where. Meanwhile
Here we are, we lean on our lives
Expecting purpose to keep her date,
Get cold waiting, watch the overworlds
Come and go, question the need to stay
But do, in an obstinate anticipation of love.
Ah, love me, it's a long misuse of breath
For boys like us. When do we start?

DAVID. When you suffering god'sbodies
Come to your senses. What you'll do
Is lose us life altogether.
Amply the animal is Cain, thank God,
As he was meant to be: a huskular strapling
With all his passions about him. Tomorrow
Will know him well. Momentous doings
Over the hill for the earth and us.
What hell else do you want?

PETER.   The justification.

DAVID. Oh, bulls and bears to that.
The word's too long to be lived.
Just if, just if, is as far as ever you'll see.

PETER. What's man to be?

DAVID.   Content and full.

PETER. That's modest enough.
What an occupation for eternity.
Sky's hollow filled as far as for ever
With rolling light: place without limit,
Time without pity:
And did you say all for the sake of our good condition,
All for our two-footed prosperity?

[173]

Well, we should prosper, considering
The torment squandered on our prospering.
From squid to eagle the ravening is on.
We are all pain-fellows, but nothing you dismay,
Man is to prosper. Other lives, forbear
To blame me, great and small forgive me
If to your various agonies
My light should seem hardly enough
To be the cause of the ponderable shadow.

DAVID. Who do you think you are, so Angel-sick?
Pain warns us to be master: pain prefers us.
Draws us up.

PETER.   Water into the sun:
All the brooding clouds of us!

DAVID.   All right.
We'll put it to the High and Mighty.
Play you dice to know who's favoured.

PETER. What's he to do with winning?

DAVID.   Play you dice.
Not so sure of yourself, I notice.

PETER. I'll play you. Throw for first throw.
Now creation be true to creatures.

ADAMS. Look, sir, my sons are playing.
How silent the spectators are,
World, air, and water.
Eyes bright, tension, halt.
Still as a bone from here to the sea.

DAVID [*playing*]. Ah-h-h-h!

[174]

ADAMS. Sir, my sons are playing. Cain's your man.
   He goes in the mould of passion as you made him.
   He can walk this broken world as easily
   As I and Eve the ivory light of Eden.
   I recommend him. The other boy
   Frets for what never came his way,
   Will never reconcile us to our exile.
   Look, sir, my sons are playing.
   Sir, let the future plume itself, not suffer.

PETER [*playing*]. How's that for a nest of singing birds?

ADAMS. Cain sweats: Cain gleams. Now do you see him?
   He gives his body to the game.
   Sir, he's your own making, and has no complaints.

DAVID. Ah! What are you doing to me, heaven and earth?

PETER. Friendly morning.

DAVID [*shaking the dice*]. Numbers, be true to nature.
                 Deal me high,
                 Six dark stars
                 Come into my sky.

                                    [*He throws.*

   Blight! What's blinding me
   By twos and threes? I'm strong, aren't I?
   Who's holding me down? Who's frozen my fist
   So it can't hatch the damn dice out?

PETER [*shaking and throwing*].
                 Deal me high, deal me low.
                 Make my deeds
                 My nameless needs.
                 I know I do not know.
   . . . That brings me home!

                 [DAVID *roars with rage and disappointment.*

[175]

DAVID. Life is a hypocrite if I can't live
   The way it moves me! I was trusted
   Into breath. Why am I doubted now?
   Flesh is my birthplace. Why shouldn't I speak the tongue?
   What's the disguise, eh? Who's the lurcher
   First enjoys us, then disowns us?
   Keep me clean of God, creation's crooked.

ADAMS. Cain, steady, steady, you'll raise the world.

DAVID. You bet your roots I will.
   I'll know what game of hide and seek this is.
   Half and half, my petering brother says,
   Nothing of either, in and out the limbo.
   'I know I do not know' he says.
   So any lion can BE, and any ass,
   And any cockatoo: and all the unbiddable
   Roaming voices up and down
   Can live their lives and welcome
   While I go pestered and wondering down hill
   Like a half-wit angel strapped to the back of a mule.
   Thanks! I'll be as the body was first presumed.

PETER. It was a game between us, Cain.

DAVID [in a fury]. Your dice were weighted! You thought you
      could trick
   The life out of me. We'll see about that.
   You think you're better than you're created!
   I saw the smiles that went between
   You and the top air. I knew your game.
   Look helpless, let him see you're lost,
   Make him amiable to think
   He made more strangely than he thought he did!
   Get out of time, will you, get out of time!
      [He takes PETER by the throat. ADAMS goes to part them.

[176]

ADAMS. Cain, drop those hands!

> [*He is wheeled by an unknown force back against his bunk.*

O Sir,
Let me come to them. They're both
Out of my reach. I have to separate them.

DAVID [*strangling* PETER]. You leave us now, leave us, you half-
and-half:
I want to be free of you!

PETER.   Cain! Cain!

ADAMS. Cain, Cain!

DAVID.   If life's not good enough for you
Go and justify yourself!

ADAMS. Pinioned here, when out of my body
I made them both, the fury and the suffering,
The fury, the suffering, the two ways
Which here spreadeagle me.

> [DAVID *has fought* PETER *back to the bed and kills him.*

O, O, O,
Eve, what love there was between us. Eve,
What gentle thing, a son, so harmless,
Can hang the world with blood.

DAVID [*to* PETER].   Oh,
You trouble me. You are dead.

ADAMS. How ceaseless the earth is. How it goes on.
Nothing has happened except silence where sound was,
Stillness where movement was. Nothing has happened,
But the future is like a great pit.
My heart breaks, quiet as petals falling
One by one, but this is the drift
Of agony for ever.

[177]

DAVID.   Now let's hope
   There will be no more argument,
   No more half-and-half, no more doubt,
   No more betrayal.—You trouble me,
   You trouble me.

MEADOWS [*in his sleep*]. Cain.

                    [DAVID *hides*

                         Cain. Where is
   Your brother?

DAVID.   How should I know? Am I
   His keeper?

ADAMS.   Where is keeping?
   Keep somewhere, world, the time we love.
   I have two sons, and where is one,
   And where will now the other be?
   I am a father unequipped to save.
   When I was young the trees of love forgave me:
   That was all. But now they say
   The days of such simple forgiveness are done,
   Old Joe Adam all sin and bone.

MEADOWS. Cain: I hear your brother's blood
   Crying to me from the ground.

DAVID. Sir, no: he is silent.
   All the crying is mine.

MEADOWS. Run, run, run. Cain
   Is after you.

DAVID.   What shall I do?

MEADOWS. What you have done. It does it to you.
   Nowhere rest. Cage of the world
   Holds your prowling. Howl, Cain, jackal afraid.

And nowhere, Cain, nowhere
Escape the fear of what men fear in you.
Every man's hand will be against you,
But never touch you into quietness.
Run! Run!

DAVID.   The punishment
Is more than I can bear. I loved life
With a good rage you gave me. And how much better
Did Abel do? He set up his heart
Against your government of flesh.
How was I expected to guess
That what I am you didn't want?
God the jailer, God the gun
Watches me exercise in the yard,
And all good neighbourhood has gone.
The two-faced beater makes me fly,
Fair game, poor game, damned game
For God and all man-hunters.

MEADOWS. They shall never kill you.

DAVID. Death was a big word, and now it has come
An act so small, my enemies will do it
Between two jobs. Cain's alive,
Cain's dead, we'll carry the bottom field:
Killing is light work, and Cain is easily dead.

MEADOWS. Run on, keep your head down, cross at the double
The bursts of open day between the nights.
My word is Bring him in alive.
Can you feel it carved on your body?

[DAVID *twists as though he felt a branding iron touch him.*

DAVID. God in heaven! The drag!
You're tearing me out of my life still living!

This can't last on flesh for ever.
Let me sleep, let me, let me, let me sleep.
God, let me sleep. God, let me sleep.

> [*He goes into the shadows to his bed.*

MEADOWS [*turning in bed*]. This can't last on flesh for ever.
Let me sleep.

> [*There follows a pause of heavy breathing. The church clock
> in the tower strikes the three-quarters.* MEADOWS *wakes,
> props himself up on his elbow.*

Any of you boys awake?
Takes a bit of getting used to, sleeping
In a looming great church. How you doing?
I can't rest easy for the night of me.
. . . Sleeping like great roots, every Jack of them.
How many draughts are sifting under the doors.
Pwhee-ooo. And the breathing: and breathing: heavy and deep:
Breathing: heavy and deep.
Sighing the life out of you. All the night.

> [DAVID *stirs uneasily.*

DAVID. I don't have to stay here! I'm a King.

MEADOWS. David, that you? You awake, David?
A dream's dreaming him. This is no place
For lying awake. When other men are asleep
A waking man's a lost one. Tim, go byes.

> [*He covers his head with his blanket.*

DAVID [*in his sleep*]. I'm King of Israel. They told me so.
I'm doing all right. But who is there to trust?
There are so many fools. Fools and fools and fools,
All round my throne. Loved and alone
David keeps the earth. And nothing kills them.

[PETER, *as the dream figure of Absalom, stands with his back pressed against a wall as though afraid to be seen.*

PETER. Do you think I care?

DAVID.   Who is that man down there
In the dark alley-way making mischief?

PETER. Do you think I care?

DAVID.   Corporal Joab:
There's a man in the dark way. Do you see
That shadow shift? it has a belly and ribs.
It's a man, Joab, who shadows me. He lurks
Against my evening temper. Dangerous.

                    [ADAMS *appears as the dream figure of Joab.*

ADAMS. I think you know already.

DAVID. He has got to be named. Which of us does it?

ADAMS. He's your own son: Absalom.

DAVID.   Now
The nightmare sits and eats with me.
He was boy enough.
Why does he look like a thief?

ADAMS.   Because
He steals your good, he steals your strength,
He riddles your world until it sinks,
He plays away all your security,
All you labour and suffer to hold
Against the enemy.

DAVID.   The world's back
Is bent and heavily burdened, and yet he thinks
He can leapfrog over. Absalom,
Absalom, why do you play the fool against me?

[181]

PETER. You and your enemies! Everlastingly
 Thinking of enemies. Open up.
 Your enemies are friends of mine.

DAVID. They gather against our safety. They make trash
 Of what is precious to us. Absalom,
 Come over here. I want to speak to you.

PETER [*running up into the pulpit*]. Do you think I care?

ADAMS.   If you let him run
 He'll make disaster certain.

DAVID.   Absalom,
 Come alive. Living is caring.
 Hell is making straight towards us.

PETER [*in the pulpit*]. Beloved, all who pipe your breath
 Under the salted almond moon,
 Hell is in my father's head
 Making straight towards him. Please forget it.
 He sees the scarlet shoots of spring
 And thinks of blood. He sees the air
 Streaming with imagined hordes
 And conjures them to come. But you and I
 Know that we can turn away
 And everything will turn
 Into itself again. What is
 A little evil here and there between friends?
 Shake hands on it: shake hands, shake hands:
 Have a cigarette, and make yourselves at home.
 Shall we say what we think of the King of Israel?
 Ha—ha—ha!

     [*Jeering laughter echoes round the roof of the church.*

[182]

DAVID. Don't do it to me, don't make the black rage
   Shake me, Peter. I tremble like an earthquake
   Because I can't find words which might
   Put the fear of man into you.
   Understand! The indecisions
   Have to be decided. Who's against us
   Reeks to God. Where's your hand?
   Be ordinary human, Absalom.

ADAMS. Appeal's no use, King. He has
   A foiling heart: the sharp world glances off
   And so he's dangerous.

DAVID.   I think so too.
   Who can put eyes in his head? Who'll do it,
   Eh, Joab? We have to show him
   This terse world means business, don't we, Corporal,
   Don't we?

ADAMS.   He has to be instructed.

DAVID. Make a soldier of him. Make him fit
   For conflict, as the stars and stags are.
   He belongs to no element now. We have
   To have him with us. Show him the way,
   Joe Adams.

       [PETER *is lounging at the foot of the pulpit.* ADAMS *turns
       to him.*

ADAMS.   Get on parade.

PETER.   What's the music?

ADAMS. I'll sing you, Absalom, if you don't get moving.
   And I'll see you singing where you never meant.
   Square up.

PETER.   What's this?

ADAMS.   Square up, I said.

PETER. Where do we go from here?

ADAMS.   It's unarmed combat.
It's how your bare body makes them die.
It's old hey-presto death: you learn the trick
And death's the rabbit out of the hat:
Rolling oblivion for someone.
You've got to know how to get rid of the rats of the world.
They're up at your throat. Come on.

PETER. What nightmare's this you're dragging me into?

ADAMS. Humanity's. Come on.

PETER.   I know
Nothing about it. Life's all right to me.

ADAMS. Say that when it comes.

                    [*The unarmed combat,* ADAMS *instructing.*

DAVID. Where is he going now? He carries
No light with him. Does he know
The river's unbound: it's up above
Every known flood-mark, and still rising.

PETER [*who has got away from* ADAMS]. I'm on the other side of the
river
Staying with friends, whoever they are.
Showery still, but I manage to get out,
I manage to get out.
The window marked with a cross is where I sleep.
Just off to a picnic with your enemies.
They're not bad fellows, once you get to know them.

DAVID [*to* ADAMS]. I have heard from my son.

ADAMS.   What's his news?

[184]

DAVID. He's with the enemy. He betrays us, Joab.
He has to be counted with them.
Are we ready?

ADAMS.　　　　　　　Only waiting for the word.

DAVID. We attack at noon.

ADAMS.　　　　　　　　Only hoping for the time.
Good luck.

DAVID.　　　　Good luck.

[ADAMS *walks down the chancel steps and crouches, keeping
a steady eye on his wrist-watch.* ADAMS *gives a piercing
whistle.* PETER *leaps up and hangs on to the edge of the
pulpit.* ADAMS *cuts him down with a tommy-gun. He cries
out.* DAVID *starts up in his bunk.* PETER *and* ADAMS *fall to
the floor and lie prone.*

[*Awake.*] What's the matter, Peter? Pete! Anything wrong?

[*He gets out of his bunk and goes across to Peter's.*

Pete, are you awake?

[*He stands for a moment and then recrosses the floor.*

MEADOWS [*awake*].　　Anything the matter?
Can't you sleep either?

DAVID [*getting back into his bunk*]. I thought I heard
Somebody shout. It woke me up.

MEADOWS.　　　　　　　　Nobody shouted.
I've been lying awake. It's just gone midnight.
There's a howling wind outside plays ducks and drakes
With a flat moon: just see it through this window:
It flips across the clouds and then goes under:
I wish I could run my head against some sleep.

[185]

This building's big for lying with your eyes open.
You could brush me off, and only think you're dusting.
Who's got the key of the crypt? [*He yawns.*]
Thanks for waking. It brings the population
Up to two. You're a silent chap. Dave?
Have you gone to sleep again already?
Back into the sea, like a slippery seal.
And here am I, high and dry.

DAVID [*asleep*]. Look, look, look.

MEADOWS.   Away he goes,
Drifting far out. How much of him is left?
Ah, lord, man, go to sleep: stop worrying.

                [ADAMS *drags or carries* PETER *to Peter's bunk.*

DAVID. Joab, is that you? Joab, is that you?
What are you bringing back?

ADAMS.   The victory.

DAVID. Are you sure it is the victory, Joab?
Are we ever sure it's the victory?
So many times you've come back, Joab,
With something else. I want to be sure at last.
I want to know what you mean by victory.
Is it something else to me? Where are you looking?
There's nothing that way. But look over here:
There's something. Along the road, starting the dust,
He wants to reach us. Why is that?
So you're going to walk away.

ADAMS [*going to his bunk*]. I've done my best.
I can't be held responsible for everything.

DAVID. Don't leave me, Joab. Stay and listen.

[186]

ADAMS [*covering himself over*]. I'm dead beat.
The enemy's put to flight. Good night, you King of Israel.

DAVID. Bathed in sweat, white with dust. Call him here.
Come up. I am the King.
I shall wait patiently until your voice
Gets back the breath to hit me. I'm here, waiting.

> [DAVID *sits on the edge of his bunk, a red army blanket*
> *hanging from his shoulder.*

MEADOWS [*awake*]. Where are you off to, Davey?
Get you back to bed. A dream
Has got you prisoner, Davey, like
The world has got us all. Don't let it
Take you in.

DAVID. Come here to me, come over
Here, the dusty fellow with the news,
Come here. Is the fighting over? Unconditionally?

> [MEADOWS *has left his bunk and crossed to* DAVID.

MEADOWS. Lie down, boy. Forget it. It's all over.

DAVID. Is the young man Absalom safe?

MEADOWS Lie down, Dave.
Everybody's asleep.

ADAMS [*from his bunk*]. The boy's dead.
You might as well be told: I say
The boy's dead.

> [DAVID, *giving a groan, lies back on his bed.*

MEADOWS. The night's over us.
Nothing's doing. Except the next day's in us
And makes a difficult sort of lying-in.
Here, let's cover you up. Keep the day out of this.
Find something better to sleep about.

[187]

Give your living heart a rest. Do you hear me,
Dave, down where you are? If you don't mind,
While I'm here, I'll borrow some of that sleep:
You've got enough for two.

[*He limps back to his bunk, passing* ADAMS, *who wakes.*

ADAMS.   Hullo, Meadows:
What's worrying you?

MEADOWS.   Dave was. He couldn't
Let go of the day. He started getting up
And walking in his sleep.

ADAMS.   All right now?

MEADOWS. Seems running smoother.

ADAMS.   Is that him talking?

[PETER *has begun to talk in his sleep.*

MEADOWS. Muttering monkeys love us, it's the other one now:
Peter's at it.

PETER.   Do I have to follow you?

ADAMS. You needn't hear him if you get your ears
Under the blankets. That's where I'm going.
Good-night, boy.

[*He disappears under his blankets.* MEADOWS *climbs into his bunk.*

MEADOWS.   Hope so. It's a choppy crossing
We're having still. No coast of daylight yet for miles.

[*He also disappears from view. A pause.*

PETER [*asleep*]. Why did you call me? I'm contented here:
They say I'm in a prison. Morning comes
To a prison like a nurse:

[188]

A rustling presence, as though a small breeze came,
And presently a voice. I think
We're going to live. The dark pain has gone,
The relief of daylight
Flows over me, as though beginning is
Beginning. The hills roll in and make their homes,
And gradually unfold the plains. Breath
And light are cool together now.
The earth is all transparent, but too deep
To see down to its bed.

     [DAVID, *the dream figure of Abraham, stands beside* PETER.

DAVID.   Come with me.

PETER. Where are we going?

DAVID.   If necessary
To break our hearts. It's as well for the world.

PETER. There's enough breaking, God knows. We die,
And the great cities come down like avalanches.

DAVID. But men come down like living men.
Time gives the promise of time in every death,
Not of any ceasing. Come with me.
The cities are pitifully concerned.
We need to go to the hill.

PETER.   What shall we do?

DAVID. What falls to us.

PETER.   Falling from where?

DAVID. From the point of devotion, meaning God.
Carry this wood, Isaac, and this coil
Of rope.

PETER.   I'm coming.

[189]

DAVID.   There has to be sacrifice.
  I know that. There's nothing so sure.

PETER. You walk so fast. These things are heavy.

DAVID. I know. I carry them too.

PETER.   I only want
  To look around a bit. There's so much to see.
  Ah, peace on earth, I'm a boy for the sights.

DAVID. Don't break my heart. You so
  Cling hold of the light. I have to take it
  All away.

PETER.   Why are you so grave?
  There's more light than we can hold. Everything
  Grows over with fresh inclination
  Every day. You and I are both
  Immeasurably living.

        [DAVID *has been walking towards the pulpit.* PETER *still lies*
        in bed. He starts to whistle a tune, though the whistling seems
        not to come from his lips but from above him.

DAVID. What do you whistle for?

PETER.   I whistle for myself
  And anyone who likes it.

DAVID.   Keep close to me.
  It may not be for long. Time huddles round us,
  A little place to be in. And we're already
  Up the heavy hill. The singing birds
  Drop down and down to the bed of the trees,
  To the hay-silver evening, O
  Lying gentleness, a thin veil over
  The long scars from the nails of the warring hearts.

[190]

Come up, son, and see the world.
God dips his hand in death to wash the wound,
Takes evil to inoculate our lives
Against infectious evil. We'll go on.
I am history's wish and must come true,
And I shall hate so long as hate
Is history, though, God, it drives
My life away like a beaten dog. Here
Is the stone where we have to sacrifice.
Make my heart like it. It still is beating
Unhappily the human time.

PETER. Where is the creature that has to die?
There's nothing here of any life worth taking.
Shall we go down again?

DAVID.   There is life here.

PETER. A flinching snail, a few unhopeful harebells.
What good can they be?

DAVID.   What else?

PETER.   You, father,
And me.

DAVID.   I know you're with me. But very strangely
I stand alone with a knife. For the simple asking.
Noon imperial will no more let me keep you
Than if you were the morning dew. The day
Wears on. Shadows of our history
Steal across the sky. For our better freedom
Which makes us living men: for what will be
The heaven on earth, I have to bind you
With cords, and lay you here on the stone's table.

PETER. Are you going to kill me? No! Father!
   I've come only a short way into life
   And I can see great distance waiting.
   The free and evening air
   Swans from hill to hill.
   Surely there's no need for us to be
   The prisoners of the dark? Smile, father.
   Let me go.

DAVID.   Against my heart
   I let you go, for the world's own ends
   I let you go, for God's will
   I let you go, for children's children's joy
   I let you go, my grief obeying.
   The cords bind you against my will
   But you're bound for a better world.
   And I must lay you down to sleep
   For a better waking. Come now.

      [*In mime he picks Isaac up in his arms and lays him across
      the front of the pulpit.*

PETER [*in his bunk*].   I'm afraid.
   And how is the earth going to answer, even so?

DAVID. As it will. How can we know?
   But we must do, and the future make amends.

PETER. Use the knife quickly. There are too many
   Thoughts of life coming to the cry.
   God put them down until I go.
   Now, now, suddenly!

DAVID [*the knife raised*]. This
   Cuts down my heart, but bitter events must be.

I can't learn to forgive necessity:
God help me to forgive it.

[ADAMS *appears as the dream figure of the Angel.*

ADAMS.   Hold your arm.
There are new instructions. The knife can drop
Harmless and shining.

DAVID.   I never thought to know,
Strange voice of mercy, such happy descending.
Nor my son again. But he's here untouched,
And evening is at hand
As clear and still as no man.

PETER.   Father, I feel
The air go over me as though I should live.

DAVID. So you will, for the earth's while. Shall I
Undo the cords?

ADAMS.   These particular. But never all.
There's no loosening, since men with men
Are like the knotted sea. Lift him down
From the stone to the grass again, and, even so free,
Yet he will find the angry cities hold him.
But let him come back to the strange matter of living
As best he can: and take instead
The ram caught here by the white wool
In the barbed wire of the briar bush:
Make that the kill of the day.

DAVID.   Readily.

PETER. Between the day and the night
The stars tremble in balance.
The houses are beginning to come to light.
And so it would have been if the knife had killed me.

[193]

This would have been my death-time.
The ram goes in my place, in a curious changing.
Chance, as fine as a thread,
Cares to keep me, and I go my way.

MEADOWS [*a dream figure*]. Do you want a ride across the sands,
Master Isaac?

PETER.   Who are you?

MEADOWS.   Now, boy, boy,
Don't make a joke of me. Old Meadows,
The donkey man, who brought you up the hill.
Not remember me? That's a man's memory,
Short measure as that. Down a day.
And we've been waiting, Edwina and me,
As patient as two stale loaves, to take you down.

PETER. But I climbed the hill on foot.

MEADOWS [*patting the bunk*]. No credit, Edwina girl, no credit.
He thinks you're a mangy old moke. You tell him
There's none so mangy as thinks that others are.
You have it for the sake of the world.

PETER. All right, she can take me down. I'm rasping tired.
My whole body's like a three days' growth of beard.
But I don't know why she should have to carry me.
She's nothing herself but two swimming eyes
And a cask of ribs.

MEADOWS.   A back's a back.
She's as good as gold while she lives,
And after that she's as good as dead. Where else
Would you find such a satisfactory soul?
Gee-up, you old millennium. She's slow,
But it's kind of onwards. Jog, jog,
Jog, jog.

[194]

PETER.   There's a ram less in the world tonight.
My heart, I could see, was thudding in its eyes.
It was caught, and now it's dead.

MEADOWS.   Jog, jog,
Jog, jog, jog, jog, jog,
Jog, jog.

PETER. Across the sands and into the sea.
The sun flocks along the waves.
Blowing up for rain of sand.
Helter-shelter.

MEADOWS.   Jog. Jog. Jog.
Donkey ride is over. In under
The salty planks and corrugated iron.
Stable for mangy mokes. Home, old girl,
Home from the sea, old Millie-edwinium.
Tie up here.

                              [*He has climbed into his bunk.*

PETER.   No eyes open. All
In sleep. The innocence has come.
Ram's wool hill pillow is hard.

          [*He sighs and turns in his bunk. The church clock strikes one.
          An aeroplane is heard flying over the church.* PETER *wakens
          and sits up in his bunk, listening.*

Is that one of ours?

MEADOWS [*his face emerging from the blankets*].
                    Just tell me: are you awake
Or asleep?

PETER.   Awake. Listen. Do you hear it?
Is it one of ours?

[195]

MEADOWS.　　　　　No question: one of ours.
　Or one of theirs.

PETER.　　　　　Gone over. Funny question:
　'Was I asleep?' when I was sitting up
　Asking you a question.

MEADOWS.　　　　　　　Dave's been sitting up
　Asking questions, as fast asleep as an old dog.
　And you've been chatting away like old knitting-needles,
　Half the night.

PETER.　　　　　What was I saying?

MEADOWS.　　　　　　　　I know all
　Your secrets now, man.

PETER.　　　　　　I wish I did.
　What did I say?

MEADOWS.　　　　Like the perfect gentleman
　I obliterated my lug-holes:
　Under two blankets, army issue.
　A man must be let to have a soul to himself
　Or souls will go the way of tails.
　I wouldn't blame a man for sleeping.
　It comes to some. To others it doesn't come.
　Troubles differ. But I should be glad
　To stop lying out here in the open
　While you underearthly lads
　Are shut away talking night's language like natives.
　We only have to have Corporal Adams
　To make a start, and I might as well
　Give up the whole idea. Oh, lord, let me
　Race him to it. I'm going under now
　For the third time.

　　　　　　　　[*He covers his head with the blankets.*

[196]

PETER.   Sorry if I disturbed you.
I'll go back where I came from, and if I can
I'll keep it to myself. Poor old Meadows:
Try thinking of love, or something.
Amor vincit insomnia.

MEADOWS.   That's enough
Of night classes. What's it mean?

PETER. The writing on the wall. So turn
Your face to it: get snoring.

MEADOWS.   Not hereabouts:
It wouldn't be reverent. Good night, then.

PETER.   Same to you.

[*They cover their heads. A pause.* ADAMS, *asleep, lies flat
on his bunk, looking down over the foot of it.*

ADAMS. Fish, fish, fish in the sea, you flash
Through your clouds of water like the war in heaven:
Angel-fish and swordfish, the silver troops . . .
And I am salt and sick on a raft above you,
Wondering for land, but there's no homeward
I can see.

[*He turns on his back.*
            God, have mercy
On our sick shoals, darting and dying.
We're strange fish to you. How long
Can you drift over our sea, and not give up
The ghost of hope? The air is bright between us.
The flying fish make occasional rainbows,
But land, your land and mine, is nowhere yet.

[DAVID, *a dream figure, comes to meet him.*

[197]

How can a man learn navigation
When there's no rudder? You can seem to walk,
You there: you can seem to walk:
But presently you drown.

DAVID. Who wants us, Corporal?

ADAMS. I wish I knew. I'm soaked to the skin.
The world shines wet. I think it's men's eyes everywhere
Reflecting light. Presently you drown.

DAVID. Have you forgotten you're a prisoner?
They marched us thirty miles in the pouring rain.
Remember that? They, they, they, they.

> [PETER *comes down towards* DAVID, *marching but ex-
> hausted. As he reaches* DAVID *he reels and* DAVID *catches
> him.*

PETER. What happens if I fall out, Dave?

DAVID. You don't fall out, that's all.

PETER. They can shoot me if they like.
It'll be a bit of a rest.

DAVID. You're doing all right.

PETER. I wouldn't know. It. Feels.
Damned. Odd. To me.

DAVID. Corporal Adams,
Man half-seas overboard!
Can you lend a hand?

ADAMS [*jumping from his bunk*]. Here I come.
Does he want to be the little ghost?
Give us an arm. Dave and I will be
Your anchor, boy: keep you from drifting
Away where you're not wanted yet.

PETER. Don't think you've got me with you.
I dropped out miles ago.

ADAMS. We'll keep the memory green.

[*They do not move forward, but seem to be trudging.*

DAVID. They, they, they, they.

ADAMS. Be careful how you step. These logs we're on
Are slimy and keep moving apart.

DAVID [*breaking away*]. Where do you think we are?
We're prisoners, God! They've bricked us in.

ADAMS. Who said you were dismissed?

PETER.   Forget your stripes
For a minute, Corporal: it's my birthday next month,
My birthday, Corporal: into the world I came,
The barest chance it happened to be me,
The naked truth of all that led the way
To make me. I'm going for a stroll.

[*He wanders down towards the lectern.*

ADAMS. Where are you going? Orders are
No man leaves unless in a state of death.

DAVID. There's nowhere to go, and he knows
There's nowhere to go. He's trying to pretend
We needn't be here.

PETER.   Don't throttle yourself
With swallowing, Dave. Anyone
Would think you never expected the world.
Listen to the scriptures:
[*As though reading the Bible.*]
        Nebuchadnezzar, hitting the news,
        Made every poor soul lick his shoes.

[199]

When the shoes began to wear
Nebuchadnezzar fell back on prayer.
Here endeth the first lesson. And here beginneth
The second lesson . . .

DAVID. I'll read the second lesson:
God drown you for a rat, and let the world
Go down without you.

PETER. Three blind mice of Gotham,
Shadrac, Meshac and Abednego:
They went to walk in a fire.
If the fire had been hotter
Their tales would have been shorter.
Here endeth——

ADAMS. Get into the ranks.

PETER. What's worrying you? We're not
On active service now. Maybe it's what
They call in our paybooks 'disembodied service':
So drill my spirit, Corporal, till it weeps
For mercy everywhere.

DAVID. It had better weep,
It had better weep. By God, I'll say
We have to be more than men if we're to man
This rising day. They've been keeping from us
Who we are, till now, when it's too late
To recollect. [*Indicating* PETER.] Does he know?

ADAMS. Shadrac, Meshac, Abednego—
We didn't have those names before: I'll swear
We were at sea. This black morning
Christens us with names that were never ours
And makes us pay for them. Named,

Condemned. What they like to call us
Matters more than anything at heart.
Hearts are here to stop
And better if they do. God help us all.

PETER. Do I know what?

ADAMS.   We are your three blind mice:
Our names are Shadrac, Meshac, and Abednego.
This is our last morning. Who knows truly
What that means, except us?

PETER.   And which of us
Knows truly? O God in heaven, we're bound
To wake up out of this. Wake, wake, wake:
This is not my world! Where have you brought me?

DAVID. To feed what you've been riding pick-a-back.

PETER. I can believe anything, except
The monster.

DAVID.   And the monster's here.

ADAMS.   To make
Sure we know eternity's in earnest.

PETER. It's here to kill. What's that in earnest of?
But the world comes up even over the monster's back.
Corporal, can we make a dash for the hill there?

ADAMS. We're under close arrest.

DAVID.   O God, are we
To be shut up here in what other men do
And watch ourselves be ground and battered
Into their sins? Let me, dear God, be active
And seem to do right, whatever damned result.
Let me have some part in what goes on
Or I shall go mad!

PETER.   What's coming now
   Their eyes are on us. Do you see them?

ADAMS. Inspection. The powers have come to look us over
   To see if we're in fettle for the end.
   Get into line.

DAVID.   What, for those devils?
   Who are they?

ADAMS.   Nebuchadnezzar and his aides.
   Do what you're told.

PETER.   Is that him with one eye?

DAVID. Are they ours or theirs?

ADAMS.   Who are we, Dave, who
   Are we? If we could get the hang of that
   We might know what side they're on. I should say
   On all sides. Which is why the open air
   Feels like a barrack square.

PETER.   Is that him
   With one eye?

ADAMS.   If we could know who we are——

DAVID. I've got to know which side I'm on.
   I've got to be on a side.

ADAMS.   —They're coming up.
   Let's see you jump to it this time: we're coming
   Up for the jump. We can't help it if
   We hate his guts.—Look out.—Party, shun!

                    [*They all come to attention.*

   The three prisoners, sir.—Party, stand
   At ease!

PETER.   Purple and stars and red and gold.
   What are they celebrating?

[202]

DAVID.   We shall know soon.

ADAMS. Stop talking in the ranks.

                              [*They stand silent for a moment.*

PETER.   What bastard language
  Is he talking? Are we supposed to guess?
  Police on earth. Aggression is the better
  Part of Allah. Liberating very high
  The dying and the dead. Freedoom, freedoom.
  Will he never clear his throat?

DAVID. He's moving on.

ADAMS.   Party, at-ten-tion!
        [*They bring their heels together, but they cannot bring their
        hands from behind their backs.*

PETER. Corporal, our hands are tied!

DAVID.   They've played their game
  In the dark: we're theirs, whoever calls us.

ADAMS. Stand at ease.

DAVID.   Our feet are tied!

PETER.   Hobbled,
  Poor asses.

ADAMS.   That leaves me without a word of command
  To cover the situation, except
  Fall on your knees.

PETER.   What's coming, Corporal?

ADAMS. You two, let's know it: we have to meet the fire.

DAVID. Tied hand and foot: not men at all!

PETER.   O how
  Shall we think these moments out
  Before thinking splits to fear. I begin

To feel the sweat of the pain: though the pain
Hasn't reached us yet.

ADAMS.   Have your hearts ready:
It's coming now.

DAVID.   Every damned forest in the world
Has fallen to make it. The glare's on us.

PETER.   Dead on.
And here's the reconnoitring heat:
It tells us what shall come.

ADAMS.   Now then! Chuck down
Your wishes for the world: there's nothing here
To charm us. Ready?

DAVID.   I've been strong.
The smoke's between us. Where are you, Adams?

ADAMS. Lost.

PETER.   Where are you, Adams?

                            [ADAMS *cries out and falls to his knees.*

DAVID. It's come to him, Peter!

PETER.   We shall know!

DAVID. Scalding God!

                            [*They, too, have fallen to their knees.*

ADAMS. What way have I come down, to find
I live still, in this round of blaze?
Here on my knees. And a fire hotter
Than any fire has ever been
Plays over me. And I live. I know
I kneel.

DAVID.   Adams.

ADAMS.   We're not destroyed.

[204]

DAVID. Adams.

PETER.   Voices. We're men who speak.

DAVID. We're men who sleep and wake.
　They haven't let us go.

PETER.   My breath
　Parts the fire a little.

ADAMS.   But the cords
　That were tying us are burnt: drop off
　Like snakes of soot.

PETER.   Can we stand?

DAVID. Even against this coursing fire we can.

PETER. Stand: move: as though we were living,
　In this narrow shaking street
　Under the eaves of seven-storeyed flames
　That lean and rear again, and still
　We stand. Can we be living, or only
　Seem to be?

ADAMS.   I can think of life.
　We'll make it yet.

DAVID.   That's my devotion.
　Which way now?

PETER.   Wait a minute. Who's that
　Watching us through the flame?

　　[MEADOWS, *a dream figure, is sitting on the side of his bunk.*

DAVID.   Who's there?

ADAMS. Keep your heads down. Might be
　Some sniper of the fire.

　　　　　　　　　　　[MEADOWS *crows like a cock.*

PETER.   A lunatic.

[205]

ADAMS [*calling to* MEADOWS]. Who are you?

MEADOWS.   Man.

ADAMS.   Under what command?

MEADOWS. God's.

ADAMS.   May we come through?

MEADOWS.   If you have
The patience and the love.

DAVID.   Under this fire?

MEADOWS. Well, then, the honesty.

ADAMS.   What honesty?

MEADOWS. Not to say we do
A thing for all men's sake when we do it only
For our own. And quick eyes to see
Where evil is. While any is our own
We sound fine words unsoundly.

ADAMS.   You cockeyed son
Of heaven, how did you get here?

MEADOWS. Under the fence. I think they forgot
To throw me in. But there's not a skipping soul
On the loneliest goat-path who is not
Hugged into this, the human shambles.
And whatever happens on the farthest pitch,
To the sand-man in the desert or the island-man in the sea,
Concerns us very soon. So you'll forgive me
If I seem to intrude.

PETER.   Do you mean to stay here?

MEADOWS. I can't get out alone. Neither can you.

But, on the other hand, single moments
Gather towards the striking clock.
Each man is the world.

PETER.   But great events
Go faster.

DAVID.   Who's to lead us out of this?

MEADOWS. It's hard to see. Who will trust
What the years have endlessly said?

ADAMS. There's been a mort of time. You'd think
Something might have come of it. These men
Are ready to go, and so am I.

PETER. But there's no God-known government anywhere.

MEADOWS. Behind us lie
The thousand and the thousand and the thousand years
Vexed and terrible. And still we use
The cures which never cure.

DAVID.   For mortal sake,
Shall we move? Do we just wait and die?

MEADOWS. Figures of wisdom back in the old sorrow.
Hold and wait for ever. We see, admire
But never suffer them: suffer instead
A stubborn aberration.
O God, the fabulous wings unused,
Folded in the heart.

DAVID.   So help me, in
The stresses of this furnace I can see
To be strong beyond all action is the strength
To have. But how do men and forbearance meet?
A stone forbears when the wheel goes over, but that
Is death to the flesh.

[207]

ADAMS.   And every standing day
    The claims are deeper, inactivity harder.
    But where, in the maze of right and wrong,
    Are we to do what action?

PETER.   Look, how intense
    The place is now, with swaying and troubled figures.
    The flames are men: all human. There's no fire!
    Breath and blood chokes and burns us. This
    Surely is unquenchable? It can only transform.
    There's no way out. We can only stay and alter.

DAVID. Who says there's nothing here to hate?

MEADOWS. The deeds, not those who do.

ADAMS. Strange how we trust the powers that ruin
    And not the powers that bless.

DAVID.   But good's unguarded,
    As defenceless as a naked man.

MEADOWS. Imperishably. Good has no fear;
    Good is itself, what ever comes.
    It grows, and makes, and bravely
    Persuades, beyond all tilt of wrong:
    Stronger than anger, wiser than strategy,
    Enough to subdue cities and men
    If we believe it with a long courage of truth.

DAVID. Corporal, the crowing son of heaven
    Thinks we can make a morning.

MEADOWS.   Not
    By old measures. Expedience and self-preservation
    Can rot as they will. Lord, where we fail as men
    We fail as deeds of time.

PETER. The blaze of this fire
　　Is wider than any man's imagination.
　　It goes beyond any stretch of the heart.

MEADOWS. The human heart can go to the lengths of God.
　　Dark and cold we may be, but this
　　Is no winter now. The frozen misery
　　Of centuries breaks, cracks, begins to move;
　　The thunder is the thunder of the floes,
　　The thaw, the flood, the upstart Spring.
　　Thank God our time is now when wrong
　　Comes up to face us everywhere,
　　Never to leave us till we take
　　The longest stride of soul men ever took.
　　Affairs are now soul size.
　　The enterprise
　　Is exploration into God.
　　Where are you making for? It takes
　　So many thousand years to wake,
　　But will you wake for pity's sake?
　　Pete's sake, Dave or one of you,
　　Wake up, will you? Go and lie down.
　　Where do you think you're going?

ADAMS [*waking where he stands*]. What's wrong?

MEADOWS. You're walking in your sleep.
　　So's Pete and Dave. That's too damn many.

ADAMS. Where's this place? How did I get here?

MEADOWS. You were born here, chum. It's the same for all of us.
　　Get into bed.

PETER [*waking*]. What am I doing here?

MEADOWS. Walking your heart out, boy.

[209]

ADAMS. Dave, Dave.

MEADOWS. Let him come to himself gentle but soon
Before he goes and drowns himself in the font.

ADAMS. Wake up, Dave.

PETER. I wish I knew where I was.

MEADOWS. I can only give you a rough idea myself.
In a sort of a universe and a bit of a fix.
It's what they call flesh we're in.
And a fine old dance it is.

DAVID [*awake*]. Did they fetch us up?

MEADOWS. Out of a well. Where Truth was.
They didn't like us fraternizing. Corp,
Would you mind getting your men to bed
And stop them trapsing round the precincts?

ADAMS. Dave, we're mad boys. Sleep gone to our heads.
Come on.

DAVID. What's the time?

ADAMS. Zero hour.

DAVID. It feels like half an hour below. I've got cold feet.

PETER. [*already lying on his bunk*] I've never done that before. I
wonder now
What gives us a sense of direction in a dream?
Can we see in sleep? And what would have happened
If we'd walked into the guard? Would he have shot us,
Thinking we were trying to get out?

MEADOWS. So you were from what you said. I could stand
One at a time, but not all three together.

[210]

It began to feel like the end of the world
With all your bunks giving up their dead.

ADAMS. Well, sleep, I suppose.

DAVID.   Yeh. God bless.

PETER. Rest you merry.

MEADOWS.   Hope so. Hope so.

[*They settle down. The church clock strikes. A bugle sounds in the distance.*

THE PLAY ENDS

GALAXY BOOKS

GALAXY BOOKS

8224